VOICES OF LIGHT

LOVE, HOPE, AND HEALING FROM THE OTHER SIDE

MAUREEN ANGELINI

Editing: Laurie Knight
Cover Design: Kristina Edstrom

PEAK PRESS

An Imprint for GracePoint Publishing (www.GracePointPublishing.com)

GracePoint Matrix, LLC
624 S. Cascade Ave, Suite 201
Colorado Springs, CO 80903
www.GracePointMatrix.com
Email: Admin@GracePointMatrix.com

SAN # 991-6032

A Library of Congress Control Number has been requested and is pending.

ISBN: (Paperback) 978-1-966346-08-1
eISBN: 978-1-966346-09-8

Books may be purchased for educational, business, or sales promotional use.
For distribution queries contact Sales@IPGbook.com
For non-retail bulk order requests contact Orders@GracePointPublishing.com
Printed in U.S.A

Table of Contents

Dedication

To my family and friends whose faith in me never wavered and gave me the confidence to complete *Voices of Light*.

To the inspirers and souls on the other side who entrusted me to deliver their interdimensional messages, I'm humbled to be your voice.

And to you, the reader, who holds this book with an open heart, ready to embrace change, may *Voices of Light* guide you toward clarity, determination, and empowerment.

In Gratitude and Love,
Maureen Angelini

Content Warning

This book contains writing that some may find disturbing, including incidents of emotional abuse, suicide, self-harm, and substance abuse.

Introduction

The structure of the book, *Wisdom from the Afterlife*, resembles a mosaic we all come across. The narrative contains a compilation of personal experiences mixed with stories from the spirit world. Some pieces shine brightly and show joy, success, reflection, and growth. Others have a darker color and symbolize setbacks and hardships. Together, the mosaic, with varying intensities, portrays a story of how personal growth often emerges from overcoming difficulties. All create a picture that mourns and celebrates the complexities of the human experience from birth to death and beyond.

My journey into the exploration of the afterlife and suicide victims started after the death of my friend Eddie. Religious teachings about suicide didn't make sense to me. I only knew of a loving God. How could He send individuals who lost hope or were tormented emotionally into the fires of hell?

Two years later I retired from thirty years in the public school system where I served as a teacher and principal. The thirst for answers to my many questions about death and beyond increased. It awakened hidden innate abilities to communicate with the invisible world. Eddie and other spirits invaded my thoughts with stories of their Earthly challenges. I did not seek these souls out.

Four talented entertainers who stunned the world with their untimely passing channeled messages through me that impact society today. Fame, money, and creative abilities couldn't eliminate the pain held in the silence of their hearts. A unique perspective on human struggles followed a life review of their human existence after transition to the other side. These souls watched individuals battle with the same baggage. A heartfelt connection with the living instigated a desire to share wisdom learned in the afterlife. Their interdimensional communication and other spirit stories offer a roadmap for navigating life's journey.

The more I revisited their interdimensional messages and absorbed the love, humility, sorrow, and guidance from these souls, the more I came to understand the timeliness of their visitations. I learned from the disembodied spirits that the unworldly perspective reveals the importance of living life without regrets and understanding which struggles are worth the fight. Too many times we engage in battles with other people or within our minds that distract us from contentment. In our final days, do these conflicts matter? The rewards of triumphing over personal challenges will deliver the deepest satisfaction and pride.

Individuals who died by suicide or drug overdose attempt to comfort and provide answers to the question of *why* for living survivors. Friends and loved ones experience a complex mixture of emotions that can include grief, betrayal, confusion, and anger. Often, those left behind blame themselves for not recognizing the pain or not doing something to help the person before their passing.

The spirit messages I received convey a deep sorrow for their final action and the pain their death caused. Communications from these souls about hope, healing, and love seek to lift the heavy burdens of guilt and pain felt by loved ones.

They did nothing wrong. My demons. Pain I couldn't release.

A steep learning curve into the realms of spirit introduced terms that became constant in my everyday life. The following expressions occur throughout my writing. I aim to provide you with the definitions I was given and that I came to understand.

- **Downloads**—Messages or information received from the spirit world, higher consciousness, universal energy fields, or intuition. Like downloads on the internet, information comes quick and without effort.

- **Channeling**—The *way* I obtain information is through spirit downloads from the afterlife. I receive messages through automatic writing, trance, or meditative states. The act of channeling resembles how we tune into a TV show or radio station. It's obtained from an external source. I don't question how, I just accept. If the communication is not positive and from the light nor serves the highest good of the living, I stop the exchange.

- **Trance State**—My conscious mind goes into deep relaxation, similar to light sleep.

- **Automatic Writing**—My hand records information heard through channeling or meditation. The pen flows across the paper without stopping, effort, or judgment. Memory of the words is usually vague, much like the memory of a dream. An event or situation may trigger a recall of the event or transmission.

- **The Collective of Souls**—Many spirits speak through the vibration of one voice. The identification of a spirit by name most likely contains the sentiments of a collective of souls.

Synchronicities led me to workshops, classes, and a renowned school of psychic and spirit development in England. Whispers in my mind grew louder and more frequent. In the Night Watchmen Channel, a collective of souls said, "Our army of soldiers march to the field to be heard by many. We wait to be heard, don't turn your back." (These words and the full channeled message are in the back of the book.)

The messages I received varied in content, consistency, and origin of source. Sometimes, I heard from the collective, and other times I heard from well-known or little-known disembodied voices. The more comfortable I became, the more messages I received. This book highlights my experience—my journey to becoming a channel for those on the other side.

The spirit entertainer who died by suicide states, "The *I* is really *we*. The *we* is just louder than a single voice. In unison we say, 'Take the time to truly care. We hide our pain under a mask.'" A young woman who died by suicide at the age of twenty-two voiced an insistent plea: "Please give him this message. He needs it now." The fiancé she left behind felt he could have prevented her death and was on his own suicide mission; she knew she could do something to stop him, and I was the one to deliver the message.

Suicide rates, alcohol, drug abuse, and mental health challenges have increased at an alarming rate among our youth (as young as ten), as well as among our veterans and senior population. People blame the increased population, COVID-19, a weak economy, social media, bullying, and several other culprits. The sad truth our society is left to grapple with: Why does even one person think their life doesn't have value?

Suicide remains a reluctant topic to discuss, much like alcohol abuse thirty years ago. The tragedy of Robin Williams's death opened a dialogue about suicide prevention, mental health stigma, and associated health issues. Statistics reveal suicide claimed the lives of over 48,000 in America during 2021.[1]

Over 700,000 people die by suicide in the world each year according to the World Health Organization. An estimated quarter-million people each year in the US survive suicide attempts, according to the American Association of Suicidology (AAS). Friends and loved ones struggle with the emotional, physical, and spiritual aftermath of this type of death or the possibility of losing someone to suicide.

My place in this complex journey has been to share what I have received, not judge or reject it. I understand the uncertainty, disbelief, and religious dogmas associated with the topic of the afterlife, mediumship, and the loving words from victims of suicide. Believe me, I did not relate to these concepts before retirement, mainly because of my religious background. My belief system taught that

---

[1] CDC https://www.cdc.gov/suicide/facts/data.html

communication with the other side was impossible at least, and perhaps even a little evil. I didn't seek this out.

I'm convinced my path took a dramatic turn after I retired in order for me to uncover and embrace my innate mediumship abilities. I didn't ask for this; this found me. This gift provided a voice for the deceased and healing and comfort to their survivors, especially those who struggled with the aftermath of a death by suicide. Channeled messages from souls brought insight into the silent struggles that individuals endure daily and pushed this book forward.

When you read the downloaded messages from the spirit world, I invite you to remain skeptical. If a chord of familiarity registers in your heart, the message may be for you.

A great many people think they are thinking when
they are merely rearranging their prejudices.
William James

The Beginning

The greatest and noblest pleasure which we have
in this world is to discover new truths, and the next
is to shake off old prejudices.
Frederick the Great

June 2008

Two **years before I retired** from the public educational system, one event hurled me out of a life of predictability and into a full-throttle roller-coaster trajectory. My life spun 180 degrees. An avalanche of questions and maze-like findings trampled my moral and core religious beliefs when a friend died by suicide.

The morning of Eddie's funeral, sniffles and hushed sobs echoed through the crowded pews of Saint Augustine Church. Pleas for God's mercy on Eddie's soul stirred the air of bewilderment.

The movie camera in my mind rewound years of memories together, which deepened the loss. When my eyes refocused on the altar, an energy in the form of a light fog appeared above the casket. In my mind I heard, "I didn't know I would cause so much pain."

An icy chill raced through my every cell.

How could this be possible? Eddie, according to the Catholic religion, would remain in hell for ending his life. Yet, I heard the words and felt Eddie's essence, his invisible presence, above his lifeless body. I glanced around the room and wondered if anyone shared my experience. Silent questions evaded logic. *Could Eddie's spirit have entered the church? Did he want me to hear his words? What just happened? Had my grief summoned the vision?* A painful sadness engulfed me.

Thoughts drifted back to five days earlier when I had learned of Eddie's death. My sister Carol and I celebrated her birthday weekend at our favorite beach town. An hour after we arrived, my cell phone rang.

"Eddie is dead," a coworker sobbed.

"What are you talking about?" I asked in disbelief. It took a moment to grasp what I heard.

After a long pause I heard, "Suicide."

I'd never lost a friend to suicide. Shock and disbelief blurred the rest of the conversation. Thoughts of Eddie's smile, family, community work, and love of children flashed through my mind. *How could this be?*

As I shared memories with my sister over the next three days, the question of why lingered and tormented my mind.

Sunday arrived and ushered me back to reality in more ways than I could have imagined.

We celebrated Carol's birthday with friends at a local restaurant, but I became less present, less focused, and more preoccupied. My mind turned restless. Thoughts focused on the following day and what it would be like to have official closure for our loss. A community would gather for support over Eddie's unexpected death. How would that go? Realizing I was not in a celebratory mood, I decided to leave the restaurant early after a friend volunteered to drive Carol back to the beach house.

"Are you okay to drive?" my sister asked as she tossed me the car keys.

"Only one glass of wine this evening. See you back at the house," I grinned and reassuringly nodded my head.

Three blocks from the restaurant and less than a mile from where we stayed, bright red and blue flashing lights bounced off my rearview mirror. It didn't take long to figure out that my sister, who had been driving my car for the past three days, had turned off my automatic headlight setting. Dusk robbed the daylight. The lack of headlights captured the attention of a police officer when we drove out of the parking structure at the same time. While I didn't feel intoxicated, the telltale smell of alcohol over the weekend oozed from my pores. There was no explaining this away. Before I knew it, the cold metal of handcuffs pinched my wrists. Fear pierced every cell in my body during the emotionally paralyzing ride to the police station.

The police released me from a holding cell in the early morning hours. Anxiety filled the next four hours before the start of my workday as a school principal. *How can I function with a mind traumatized from the recent events of suicide compounded by the humiliation of an arrest and little sleep?*

The two-hour early morning drive back to town felt longer than usual. When I parked the car at school, memories of the previous night's drama faded as my years of routine and experience kicked in. The tragic loss of my friend, an administrative colleague and respected member of our community, jolted me back to the present moment.

No one at school learned about my humbling experience; only family members knew about the arrest. Fortunately, I did not lose my job and continued to work for two more years until I retired. The possibility of educational consulting after retirement turned into a lost dream. A job as a school consultant would require me to fill out an application and verify my qualifications for the position, which entailed traveling. The humiliation I felt about the arrest for driving under the influence (DUI) kept me from pursuing the position.

Apparently, the universe and the world of spirit had other plans for me.

The events that followed Eddie's death and my arrest hurled me into a foreign realm that defied logic. I started to experience atmospheric fluctuations in my ear, much like what I felt during altitude changes while in an airplane or driving in the mountains. I noticed—or sensed—flashes or objects in my peripheral vision and I would sometimes encounter what I can only describe as an edginess I didn't recognize. This left me wondering about my physical health, my sanity.

Until this point, I rarely remembered dreams or paid any attention to them until words started to repeat, repeat, *repeat* in the twilight stage before full consciousness. The repetition of the words caused an immediacy and slight awareness, enough to urge me to write them down like it was something I *had* to do. So I did.

One of my first experiences occurred with the words *Angel Therapy*. After the third repetition of the two words, I reached for paper and a pencil on the nightstand before those words slipped from my memory. Sleepiness disappeared. My curiosity about what the words meant turned into a web search that would change the course of my life.

The Angel Therapy practice, founded by Doreen Virtue, guided people to explore the spiritual gifts of healing and psychic abilities in concert with the angels and archangels. The coincidence of the exact words heard in a dream and a local workshop on angels and intuitive abilities couldn't be ignored. I knew about the angelic realm but didn't understand its relationship with psychic abilities. Despite my religious upbringing, I couldn't deny unexplainable events were unraveling at a steady pace. The timeliness of the Angel Therapy workshop piqued my interest.

Two weeks later, I attended my first paranormal course taught by the founder's son, Charles Virtue. The weekend Angel Therapy class exposed me to the terms of mediumship and channeling, along with techniques to open my senses to receive and trust what comes through.

Research into the field of mediumship led me to discover James Van Praagh. He was hailed as a pioneer and dedicated medium and evidential teacher in the mediumship movement. Coincidence struck again. Van Praagh was teaching a five-day workshop in three weeks, only a few hours from where I lived. Under the guidance of this master teacher, I gained knowledge about chakras, meditation, how to connect with the invisible world through my six senses, psychic protection, and the importance of regular development circles. I brimmed with excitement as I ventured down this path uncovering gems along the way.

My ability to hear and feel the presence of spirits and angels felt natural from the very beginning. I attributed this to my Catholic roots. Prayer and talking to God, the angels, saints, and departed loved ones started in childhood. But when I pinned the label of *mediumship* on a familiar pattern, insecurities and doubts became constant companions.

I often wondered why spirits chose me to deliver their messages. I believe Eddie's spirit visitation and words at his funeral mass unlocked the door and pushed me toward the next chapter of my journey. Other spirit communications followed and spotlighted the importance of letting go of past hurts; exercising authenticity, forgiveness, and worthiness; releasing unwanted habits or addictions; and healing.

My life changed. The frozen surfaces of my mind—the parts that held tight to a rigid societal expectation—began to thaw. Rain fell and nourished the ground with awareness and transformations. Deep appreciation for being the recipient of these insightful spirit words ignited prayers of gratitude for the honor. Synchronicities stripped bandages off old wounds and allowed emotional healing to take place. I was transformed.

Eight Years Later, November 2016

After the completion of the first draft of this manuscript in October 2015, a writer friend, Marilyn, and I registered for a year-long master class on marketing strategies. We welcomed a three-day intensive workshop with curiosity, hope, and eagerness.

At the end of the first day, brain-dead and exhausted, Marilyn and I collapsed on our hotel beds before the door closed. We came to the realization that the latest advances in technology and business communications were hurtles that resembled hard labor for two elderly women.

As we reflected on the day, Marilyn couldn't help but consider the speaker's lead-in question and how it had grabbed the audience's attention. "Maureen, what's your opinion of his question: 'How many of you attempted suicide or seriously considered it?'"

"I agree with you. He knew how to get the group's attention," I responded.

Marilyn continued, "I must say I was a bit surprised. Even he, a prominent business CEO, answered his own question with a raised hand. Kind of hesitant to look around, I had the impression many hands went up. With trepidation, I peeked over my shoulder and was shocked at the number of people who raised their hands. Maybe your book will have an audience."

Marilyn's tone changed from exhausted to inquisitive. "Maureen, why is this topic so important to you? You didn't raise your hand."

"The subject always seemed dark and forbidden, especially by religious standards. Eddie's death changed my perception. His telepathic words of anguish, '*I didn't mean to cause so much pain*,' haunts me. How can I ignore the suicide statistics, downloads from spirit, and the tortured minds of survivors?"

The temperature in the room rose along with my voice. Nervous, I felt this might be a good chance for me to explore and process what happened.

"I recently attended my first Catholic conference. A religious nun addressed the topic of suicide in one of the sessions. Like me, most people in the room were not aware of the 1983 Canon Law that changed concerning suicide. The church finally understands that the causes of suicide are complex. It now acknowledges that in many of these deaths, people struggled with emotional stress, depression, fear, anxiety, and several other factors known only to them and God. The nun referred to Jesus and the story of the Good Shepard when she said, 'Although a loved one slipped through our hands, he or she is now held in the loving arms of God.' Muffled sobs were heard throughout the conference room."

"Marilyn, I welcomed updates in the Church's attitude. Survivors struggle enough without the additional shame and thoughts that their loved one's soul will be forever damned."

Marilyn's slack body shifted on her bed into a more alert position on her side. With a fixed, analytical stare, she asked, "Have you ever thought of suicide?"

I shook my head from side to side. "No." I stared at the wall in front of me in the same manner that I would have watched a scene from a movie.

The silence in the room transported my mind to a hypnotic state. I said, "I remember when I was twenty-one, I just wanted to go away. The word *suicide* never entered my thoughts. I felt disconnected from emotions and reality, like I was maybe living someone else's story; it was surreal."

"What happened?"

"I don't recall much in the weeks before that night, only what I planned. After my husband fell asleep, I walked into my nine-month-old son's room and changed my clothes. I remember that I watched my baby boy sleep. He was so beautiful and peaceful. I kissed his soft cheek. I put an envelope on the dressing table and turned off the lamp. Blinded by the house's darkness, I slowly maneuvered through the living room. Steps from the front door, I stumbled over a wooden car. I picked up the toy, cradled it, fell to the floor, and sobbed. It triggered forgotten emotions."

"I don't understand how you could even *think* about ending your life without regard for your baby and husband."

A numbness washed over me. I questioned my own memory while speaking aloud, "Just a bad dream? I don't think so. I experienced tremendous love and protectiveness for my son after he was born. I'd never experienced this type of happiness or peace. It also fed the obsessive fear I might lose him. I couldn't let that happen. My emotions turned to emptiness."

Silence.

"Marilyn, you're the first person to ask me if I ever considered suicide. The memory of that night left a scar of guilt, too painful to remember or admit, even to myself."

After that day, when I just wanted to go away, life evolved amid challenges, lessons, joys, and love.

The only person you are destined to become is the
person you decide to be.
Ralph Waldo Emerson

Chapter 1

Leaving Too Soon

I didn't mean to cause so much pain and sorrow.
Eddie

2013

For years, I resisted the practice of meditation and proclaimed, "My life is too busy to sit and do nothing." I rejected doctors' advice and comments from well-meaning friends. High-impact exercise routines and extended hours as a principal stuffed painful childhood recollections into a cold corner of my heart. After thirty years in the public school system, I retired. The shield of busyness crumbled. Divine timing marched in its place.

On the steep climb up the mountain of self-awareness, all signs broadcasted the importance of mindfulness. It apparently heals the body and mind to produce inner peace and wisdom without cost. In short, it's been hailed as a miracle for centuries. *I have nothing to lose except time,* I reasoned.

The practice of mind stillness sharpened my senses within two months. Words surfaced in my mind that belonged to other people. Images and smells, not present in the physical world, appeared at random times and during meditations. I recorded everything—without judgment—in my journal. Often, I would read over my entries and have absolutely no recollection of having experienced or written about these unusual events. I began to voraciously explore what I could to find out more.

Exploration of various meditation methods led me to find a routine that replicated the serenity I experienced in church. A dedicated time for practice initiated an unquenchable anticipation and inner excitement. A light peppermint essential oil spray mixed with holy water opened the room as part of my preparation ritual. This provided an uplifting aroma and cleansed the space for me, readying it—and me—to accept what would follow. Soft, ambient music played in the background. A flickering white candle delivered light into the semi-dark room; a sense of quiet power radiated from its simplicity and beauty. For my protection in a semi-altered state of mind, I invoked Archangel Michael and his protective band of angels to surround the room and banish any form of energy that did not reside in the light of God. I placed a notebook and pen on the table to jot down thoughts and inspirations during the session.

The evening of July 31, 2013, started in the same manner. Thoughts faded as I relaxed. Gradually, sensations of feathery touches traveled down each side of my face and progressed into chilly tingles throughout my body. Eddie's name echoed in my mind. Silent questions erased the stillness of the moment. The flame of the candle swirled and bobbed with untamed enthusiasm. Anxiety intertwined with placidity. Deep breathing and the repetition of a prayerful mantra calmed my heartbeat and lured me back into semi-alertness.

Words grew louder in my mind. Without hesitation, I reverted to years of note-taking in a learner's environment and transcribed words that raced through my mind.

They yearn for answers
There are none, only a fear that grips the soul and shatters life
I cannot see any more but the darkness of fear and pity
The darkness in the pit of our belly becomes the ruler
All emotions and thoughts reside in this darkness
Only when we leave this plane do we see the light and love left behind
The mind yells out in pain for what we see in the ones left to pick up the

pieces
Their cries pierce our souls a thousand times more than the pain we
thought we knew
Their tears are lessons to be learned and reviewed
Help wipe the pain from their hearts, the tears from their cheeks
Tell them I love them more than they can imagine
I am sorry
Let them know I am okay and always around
I didn't mean to cause so much pain and sorrow
It belongs to me, not to them
They did nothing wrong
Fear distorts all rationalization
Carry the lantern of light into the hearts of those I hurt
Help the light of the lantern bring the beginning of hope and peace in
their heart

Dazed and confused, I placed the pen on the table when the transmission ended. I stared at the notebook. Moments later, my eyes focused on the words.

Five years after my friend Eddie's suicide, I recognized the possibility that Eddie's spirit communicated telepathically with me. Was this an attempt to answer questions that tormented the minds of loved ones and friends left behind?

The thought of Eddie not in hell brought a sense of relief. After I read the passage a few more times, I started to process the pain souls feel when they view the consequences of their final acts on Earth. I believe the spirit's words, "Their tears are lessons to be learned and reviewed," refer to a review of their life after death. Individuals who have had near-death experiences (NDEs) give similar statements. I recall reading many of these as I delved into this topic: "My life flashed before me." "All our actions and words affect the world around us." "We don't understand the ripple effect of our behavior until we transition to the next realm of existence." "Excuses only exist on the Earthly plane."

The pain and regrets expressed throughout Eddie's download made me reevaluate my thoughts on suicide. *Do any of us have the right to judge another?* During life, Eddie's quiet strength and confidence nourished others. He enjoyed and valued people and family. Through the words of spirit, we learn that challenges and struggles changed Eddie's world; they remained private, consumed his thoughts, and invaded rational behavior.

The more I read the spirit communication, the clearer it became that the last two lines in the download were directed toward me. The spirit needed me to deliver this message. My logical mind yelled, *How?*

If I didn't understand the process of my unconscious surrender to the invisible world, why would grieving family members take me seriously? Yet my heart told a different story. The passion, sorrow, and personal reflections throughout this interdimensional trans-mission provided a chance to bring healing and closure to loved ones.

I eventually found the courage to share Eddie's afterlife com-munication with his wife, Stacy. My ego and pride stepped aside; this wasn't about me. A departed soul needed my help to say, "I'm sorry."

Stacy's *hello* on the phone initiated a nervous babble from me about the reason for my call.

Silence.

"Would you like to hear the message I received?"

"Yes."

Tears blurred my vision when I heard and felt the emotion behind gentle sobs, two-thirds through her husband's spirit words.

"Thank you for sharing this with me. I appreciate your call. We've moved on and forgave Eddie a few years ago."

The years between Eddie's first spirit visitation in the church, "I didn't know I'd cause so much pain," and this recent communication began to unravel beliefs I once held sacred. Synchronicities and conversations hinged around two topics: suicide and the afterlife. As I prayed and meditated, I realized my life and retirement plans had changed. Another field of study emerged. This led to research on the afterlife, death, electromagnetic energy, and the heart connection of souls, both living and dead.

When I reflect on my early classes within the paranormal arena, spirit whispers originated in an organic manner, without effort on my part. I began to hear, see, feel, sense, and smell in ways that defied common sense but simultaneously felt natural. It created a knowingness. When the mind or ego's volume increased, doubts crept in and challenged my newfound abilities. Most of the time, the velocity of a thirsty curiosity and focused drive overruled my fears and insecurities.

Eddie's Spirit Messages to the Living

The first five lines of the download provide a glimpse into Eddie's emotions before he ended his life. The spirit tells us that the darkness of fear and self-pity sabotages thoughts and behavior.

In the afterlife, spirits observe the pain, tears, guilt, and sorrow in those they left behind: "Their cries (the living) pierce our souls a thousand times more than the pain we thought we knew."

I believe the purpose of this transmission is to convey the sentiments of Eddie's soul. We feel bad when we unintentionally hurt someone, especially those we love. There's a choice to undo the damage caused by our actions or words. In this case, Eddie's spirit lost the option to personally tell loved ones, "I'm sorry, it's not your fault. This belongs to me."

"I'm okay. I love you and am always around"
becomes the mantra of the deceased.

In the weeks that followed Eddie's recent download, a barrage of multi-layered questions surfaced: *What triggered his suicidal thoughts?*

The following interdimensional communication revealed the meaning behind Eddie's downloaded phrase: *Fear distorts all rationalization.* These spirits exposed insights beyond textbook research and individual philosophies on suicide which delve into the humanness and fragile balance between fear and hope.

Chapter 2
The Sea of Life Channel

A Rare View of Suicide, Described by Souls from the Other Side

Two weeks after I recorded Eddie's spirit message in meditation, I received the Sea of Life download. The spirit authors of this message, The Collective Voice and One Voice, offered a profound perspective on the emotions before ending one's life. Channeled words compare a person's feelings of despair to someone lost at sea.

I believe this interdimensional communication was not intended to be a voyage into the darkness of the mind. The spirit authors didn't seek pity, instead they sought to release the guilt in the minds and hearts of those left behind.

Spirit Messages to the Living
from a Collective of Souls

The Collective Voice represents a unified voice of souls who died by suicide.

Their message to the survivors:

- *Thoughts of suicide don't exist in the early phase of a life challenge or struggle.*

- *When fears rule, emotions change. Reality blurs.*

- *Images of family members fade under the weight of dread and uncertainties.*

Spirit Message to the Living
from an Individual Soul

An individual soul named One Voice attempts to answer the question of why. The download indicated it was a personal journey:

- *When numbness surrounds the person, the cries for help weaken, then vanish.*

- *Fears act like sharks. They prey on the mind and then attack sensible thoughts.*

- *A battle between despair and hope emerges.*

- *An emptiness invades all emotions: Nothing is real anymore. Reason evaporates.*

The Sea of Life download provides insight into suicide prevention. It's an intimate look at emotions and brings awareness to individuals who silently struggle to cope before reality slips from their grip. The best chance for intervention occurs before detachment or despair.

August 13, 2013, 4:57 AM

I opened my eyes, careful not to move. My pulse raced. Was someone in the room? A feeling of claustrophobia forced my body into an upright position. I switched on the light; *only me. It must have been a dream*, I concluded.

I started to drift back into sleep when an edginess and unconscious desire to write caused me to grab a pen and paper on the nightstand. I heard the words, "The Collective Voice." Through tired eyes, my hand robotically scribed across blurred, indistinct journal pages to record a surge of words heard in my mind. A semi-trance state followed.

The Collective Voice

Come, we invite all to take a journey and travel with us as we explore the minds of souls through a veil of sadness, hopelessness, self-pity, lost time, and perspective.
This journey is never really planned
We try to survive the vast dark ocean of dullness and fear
Our loved ones ride the waves in the background of our thoughts
They become more and more out of our reach
Our thoughts dodge through land mines
We try desperately to survive the violent waves of emotions
A strange form of calmness takes over, emotions and fears fade
The deafness of our thoughts emerges
An undercurrent swallows all reality from our being
This is the calmness before the storm.

The air and energy in the room turned quiet and solemn. In my mind, I saw a cloudy image move forward and identify himself as One Voice. I felt the following interdimensional words reflect the sentiments of a person before ending his life:

It is during the eye of calmness that hope or numbness is briefly allowed
Realization starts to take hold of the emotions,
A false sense of security transforms into the loneliness and hopelessness
of my surroundings
I float further and further away into the dark lonely waters of the sea
I get a glimpse, if only in my mind's eye, of sharks starting to circle
below the surface
My fears become real
I float deeper into the ocean of my mind
The thought of being rescued is entertained far less as I drift further and
further away from the shore of reality
The only refuge of thought is that the others are behind, safe from the
revenge of the lonely, dark ocean
This is my journey to find safety as I float helplessly in the shadows of
darkness and turbulence
Brief moments of calmness turn violent
My safety net crashes into another wave of emotions transmitting
despair deeper into my loins
My hope of being rescued diminishes as the turbulence wrenches to my
very core
I try to keep the slippery edge from being torn from my hand
Brief scenes in my life, of loved ones, flash before me, making my body
ache to a degree of hopelessness
A deadening numbness transcends my being, nothing is real anymore
The flight of freedom is the only escape
Pain and emotions are robbed from the body
A sea of life swallows the breath of hope

Depression and mental illness cause many self-inflicted deaths. Even if you don't accept or believe the spirits' downloaded messages, could numbness, loneliness, and despair contribute to the more than 48,500 suicides each year in America and 700,000 worldwide? (CDC and WHO)

- Suicide is the second leading cause of death worldwide for ages 15-24 years.

- Suicide is the fourth leading cause of death for adults ages 18-65 (CDC).
- Death by suicide in the teen and veteran populations increases at an alarming rate each year.
- Every forty seconds, someone in the world takes their life (WHO).
- In the U.S., there is one death by suicide every eleven minutes (CDC).

There are twenty-five attempts for every death by suicide. Around 1,200,000 people each year try to end their lives but fail, according to the US Suicide Prevention Resource Center.

Suicide may be a personal choice, but it affects family, friends, coworkers, and acquaintances.

Questions to Ponder

Have you lost someone to suicide or substance abuse?

What would you say to them if they were standing beside you?

What are three descriptive words to describe your pain after a suicide?

Have you had thoughts of suicide or that life was not worth living?

Who would be most affected by your early death?

How would this change the lives of those left behind?

Do you think the person who chose early death by suicide, alcohol, or substance abuse realized its effect on the survivors?

Did any words from Eddie or the Sea of Life downloads impact or resonate with you? How or why?

It is hopelessness even more than pain
that crushes the soul.
William Styron

Life Review and Growth in the Afterlife

My cousin Patrick appeared in a dream five months after Eddie's funeral. His spirit affirmed reports of mediums and near-death experiencers regarding a soul's growth in the afterlife. Souls evaluate their life on Earth as it flashes before them. This is often referred to as a life review.

Patrick died of a heart attack a year before the dream visitation. His life had turned downward after his mother passed during his junior year of high school and his brother's death from suicide two years later. Drugs and alcohol filled the empty hole in his heart. His life followed a self-destructive course, a slow suicide, over the next thirty years.

In my dream, I sat on a high bleacher in an auditorium and looked down at a brilliantly lit stage. I watched a blond, impeccably dressed young man proudly stroll across the stage and accept an award. He turned, looked up and smiled at me. *Patrick?* I heard him say, "Tell Judy I'm okay and I'm sorry."

A persistent urge nagged at me to call Judy, Patrick's sister, the following day. This feeling quickly changed to reluctance as I listened to my ego's chatter.

Due to busy schedules, Judy and I hadn't spoken in nearly a year. I surmised a devoted Catholic and logical person would dismiss my words. I could hear her say, "It was only a dream, nothing else." Doubts and pride changed my mind. The call could wait.

Within a minute of the decision, my eyes started to water. Chills held me hostage. An inner knowing assumed these reactions wouldn't stop until I called my cousin. Nervous fingers dialed her number. Judy's voice triggered the words from Patrick's spirit to gush from my mouth.

A prolonged silence.

"It's strange. Yesterday, an old buddy of Patrick's called. Unaware of his death, he asked how Pat was doing. Now your call, out of the blue, about a message you received in a dream that he's okay and happy." She may have received my message with trepidation or considered it coincidence, but I knew I had done the right thing.

A workshop, a year later, led by English medium Mavis Pittilla, revealed a deeper meaning for my dream. The tutor shared her opinion of a soul's growth on the other side. After a life review of challenges and successes, the spirit travels through "The World within Worlds." This resembles classrooms of learning for the soul's evolution. Patrick's smile, pride, and recognition on stage symbolized this growth. His spirit wanted us to know he's changed and is happy. The luminous image of Patrick's spirit-dream visitation remains vivid in my brain.

I feel Patrick's spirit manipulated circumstances and arranged his friend's call to Judy the day before my dream. This made it easier for his sister to consider and possibly accept her brother's message from the other side.

A reference to this concept comes from Eddie's spirit: "Their tears are lessons to be learned and reviewed."

Chapter 3

The Magnolia Tree

The Earthly journey encounters lessons and challenges. These turn into gems for self-discovery. Until polished with reflection, care, and love, they appear flawed. How we react determines our happiness.

Fifteen Years Earlier, January 1994

Aggressive rainclouds pushed the remaining light from the afternoon sky during an unusually cold January. Long strides across the backyard fueled my determination to get this task completed. I knelt on the cold, damp grass beneath the magnolia tree I had planted years earlier in memory of my grandmother.

I dug a deep hole and emptied the contents of my bucket. Pictures and mementos of my mother—including her catechism book—filled the burial site. These items triggered emotional memories, anger, and pain.

The strength of the tree's branches and the fragrance from the oversized white flowers always brought memories of Grandma's love, beauty, and protectiveness. She's been the guardian of secrets.

"Grandma, I'm sorry. I can't deal with these reminders anymore."

Two Years Before Retirement, August 2007

The 101-degree evening temperature fed my agitation while my sister and I sat in her car and watched people stagger into the building for the first DUI-mandated class of the new session. I tried to control the overpowering flight response I was having and ordered myself to breathe and calm down. Reminders of the handcuffs, jail cell, and quieting sorrow with the comfort of alcohol still quicken my pulse when I think of the weekend after I heard of Eddie's passing.

"I'll be the grandmother of the group. I can't do this; maybe next week."

"It's thirty hours of class or jail time for contempt of court," Carol reminded me.

Ten minutes later, I threw open the car door. "Please don't be late!"

Red-faced, eyes focused on the floor, I slid into the last available seat in the class, directly in front of the instructor.

The teacher's quick introduction revealed that he had retired as an undercover police officer. A mundane, fifteen-minute description of class regulations and guidelines increased my anxiety.

A commanding voice change and the "WHY" written in gigantic letters on the blackboard refocused the group's attention.

"I'd like each person to introduce yourself and tell us why you're in class this evening."

The person next to me stole my answer. "Bad luck."

"Please explain in more detail why your arrest was bad luck." The unnerving grin on the officer's face instinctively told me I needed another response.

Within a minute, all eyes focused on me. "Hello, my name is Maureen. I'm here because I started drinking after I heard of a friend's suicide."

"Why were you driving?"

"I thought I was okay."

The retired officer's intrusive eye contact felt like an invasion of privacy. Sparks of vulnerability crept through my veins.

The subsequent three sessions of the class focused on the onion effect of the three-letter, dreaded, power word: *Why*. A mounting discomfort started to torch the mental shield that supported my exterior strength.

"Most people have a pink elephant standing in the center of their lives. Your homework assignment is to describe your pink elephant."

Tightness in my chest and lightheadedness forced me to sit down after I returned home. The last few days were long. Student schedules, staff meetings, and daily operations needed finalization before teachers returned from summer break in five days. The effort to ensure a supportive, high level of morale absorbed all my energy until three hours ago. Now, I need to find the pink elephant in my personal life.

I stared at the writing assignment from the evening class. Tears welled in my eyes as memories slammed into my consciousness. The scene of a four-year-old child crouched between the refrigerator and her grandparents' house wall replaced all other thoughts.

"Don't let her take me home!" I sobbed.

"Shh honey, you made Mommy cry, too. She feels sad you won't go home with her." Shaking my head hysterically from side to side, I backed deeper into the corner. "Mommy will come back in the morning. You can stay here with us tonight."

The front door closed. Kneeling with outstretched arms, tears flowed down my grandma's cheek. She coaxed me into her arms.

"Maureen, you mustn't act like this. Your mommy loves you. She's crying, too."

It's my first vivid memory of fear mixed with guilt. Over the next few years, Grandma's comforting words, hugs, and excuses for her daughter's alcohol rages and anger erased the uncertainties or sadness.

"Honey, your mother loves you. She's upset and not feeling well."

Seven years later, this belief shattered. I remember the day I followed my mother down the narrow hallway of our house, crying, "Mommy, I love you. I love you."

In an alcoholic rage, she turned and screamed, "*I don't love you, never have!*"

Her smirk turned into a mocking laugh as I ran from room to room, trying to escape the taunting noise that ricocheted off the walls.

How much resentment or lack of emotional attachment did I pick up by age four? The heart seeks love and attention, regardless of age.

Children from dysfunctional families cultivate survival skills that twist and turn. Unhealthy patterns that seek acceptance develop. Acknowledgment of emotions or situations that shape behavioral reactions takes time, understanding, honesty, and work.

The ideal man bears the accidents of life with
dignity and grace, making the best of the
circumstances.
Aristotle

Chapter 4

Australian Necklace

Australia 1996

"One more week and we're headed back to California," my cousin Laurie reminded me.

"I like it here and don't want to leave. I've arranged a conference with the headmaster of a local private school to observe the students and check the curriculum. A principal exchange program between the two countries may be possible. Won't know unless I ask." My thoughts of making this beautiful place a temporary home had given me the courage to set up a meeting.

Laurie let out a slow, deep sigh. "I'm fully aware this is your first vacation. Staying in Australia at my sister's three-story beachfront house is a dream getaway. After a vacation, Maureen, people go home and resume their normal lives."

"Your youngest sister, Gayla, didn't. She remained in Australia after her first visit five years ago. There's something magical about this country."

"Could it be that you're not buried in work and are actually enjoying life?" Her question wasn't entirely off base; I had been consumed by work for many years and had not vacationed as some do.

"Don't know. Just feels different." Though my response was short—quipped even—I felt a stirring of something I couldn't quite articulate.

The three weeks in Queensland passed quickly. Early morning beach walks, visits to lush mountain rainforests, the outback bushland, and creeks hidden under overgrown trees filled our days. My two cousins and I sipped wine in the evenings and watched the sun melt into the ocean. Exaggerated memories delivered endless entertainment.

One night, while huddled around the fire pit, Gayla's eyes met mine for a long moment. She said in a low, controlled voice, "When will you forgive your mom? She's been dead for twenty-eight years."

Laurie shifted in her seat. Her smile disappeared. My cousin's expression told me this would be the new topic. I opened my mouth to speak, closed it, and shrugged my shoulders.

"Something needs to change. You can't keep living like this. It isn't healthy," Gayla continued.

"What are you talking about? What does my mother have to do with my life now?" Truly, I believed that chapter was closed, over.

"Everything. You hide behind your job and don't deal with emotions outside of your school." My well-meaning cousin's words cut hard, but was she on to something? I really wasn't sure.

"My work is important to me."

"Maureen, it's a job, you're replaceable. Your family needs you too." Gayla's demeanor softened. "We love you and want to help."

For the next week, bursts of blunt nagging centered on the dire necessity to forgive my mother. Torn emotions and self-talk triggered a mental fog. *Did I really need to forgive her? Was I carrying something around that I hadn't even acknowledged?*

Forty-eight hours before our check-in at the airport, I conceded. Perhaps the underlying reason for the trip *was* the forgiveness of my mother. I marched up to the third-floor deck that overlooked the ocean. Dark hues of blue clouds sailed across the sky and erased the golden-red glow of the sleepy sun. The air echoed warnings of chilly days ahead. A drift of saltwater mist felt cool and dewy across my face.

The sun's departure into the western sky always casts a spell of peace and serenity. It seemed the perfect time to change my attitude about Mother. A heaviness in my chest strengthened my resolve to let go of negative memories. I walked to the rails of the deck, raised my arms in a V shape toward the universe, and surrendered.

"Mommy, I forgive you. I want you back in my life."

Despite a feeling of relief and lightness from the previous evening's private revival ceremony, a subtle agitation crept through my senses. My mind wandered and challenged the ability to listen, follow a conversation, or speak. I started to fidget and couldn't sit or stand still. The bright, expansive living area narrowed and caused the air to feel stuffy despite the sea breeze circulating from the open glass doors.

Laurie asked with concern, "Something bothering you?"

"Must be last-day remorse, or maybe I don't want to tackle the task of packing," I responded with a chuckle.

"Makes sense to me." I was glad she didn't press for more.

Thirty minutes of stacking clothes in two massive suitcases increased my restlessness. An urge to revisit the local metaphysical store grew stronger and muffled rational thoughts.

"Maureen, the shop is two miles down the beach. It'll be dark soon."

"I won't be long." I couldn't possibly explain the pull I felt.

Laurie overheard us and yelled from her room, "We were at that place a week ago and again yesterday! There are many of those places in California."

"Be back soon," I said with a plastic smile while I hurried down the house steps to the beach.

A glance around the Mystical Homeland Store satisfied my curiosity and allowed me to keep money in my pocket.

Before I reached the door to leave, the plump, middle-aged shop owner called out, "Nice to see you again. Can I help you find something?"

"Thank you, just wanted to see if I…"

A shiny object in the jewelry case grabbed my attention.

"Is this medallion new? Didn't notice it before."

"A lady dropped the necklace off yesterday for resale."

29

The woman draped the necklace over her hand. An intricate antique silver casing complimented the oval-shaped, deep-red-black stone.

"It's unique. I like it. But just browsing today."

"Before you go, let me see how it looks on you."

She closed the silver clasp and let the chain fall on my neck. Instantly, I grabbed the object and pulled it away from my throat. "It's choking me."

"It's not touching your neck, the stone rests on your chest bone," the shop owner assured me. "Here's a mirror. The necklace delivers a strong statement. It's gorgeous on you."

"It's different," I responded while my hands tried to erase the sensation around my throat. I mentally blamed the skin sensitivity on my tiredness.

"Honey, I need to close the store now. Wear the necklace home. If it's still uncomfortable tomorrow, bring it back and I'll refund your money."

Thoughts froze. I couldn't respond. Reality and time became distorted.

My cousins' frantic reaction jolted me back to the present moment when I entered the house. "We've been worried. You left over two hours ago. What happened? Did you get lost?"

"I'm sorry. Took a different route back. Just lost track of time," I responded while tugging at the chain around my neck.

Staring at my new piece of jewelry, Gayla commented, "I like your necklace. The stone sparkles and catches the eye." Laurie smiled and nodded in agreement.

"It appeared irresistible until the shop's owner put the chain around my neck. Felt tight and heavy."

"Why did you buy it?"

"I can return it tomorrow if it's still uncomfortable."

Laurie glanced at her sister and shook her head. "We'll be at the airport when the store opens." The mounting tension warned me to keep my thoughts to myself.

"Still need to pack, join you later," I mumbled. A wave of exhaustion washed over me.

An hour later, Gayla yelled from the kitchen, "Cousin, take a break! Join us for a glass of wine and a quick stroll under the stars and moonlight."

"Leave me alone!" A harsh guttural response bellowed from my mouth. I heard the slam of the patio door. *What just happened? That wasn't me.* Shaken and confused, I crumbled to the floor. My head moved from side to side in denial.

The next morning, I descended the stairs in slow motion, determined to hold back tears and present a cheerful attitude. I greeted both cousins with sincere and tight hugs. "So sorry." I didn't know how to explain the outburst. No excuse would remove yesterday's memories. Fresh coffee aroma and cream-cheese-filled pastries canceled day-old anxieties.

On the way to the airport, our conversation supported the bond and love that had matured over the past three weeks. The words Laurie spoke one week ago replayed a different melody in my head. I now understood the meaning of a vacation. Gayla turned around in her seat to make eye contact with me when we stopped at our destination.

"It wasn't your voice last night. I don't know what happened, but it wasn't you."

Tears welled up in my eyes, "Thank you."

Laurie reached for my hand. "Let's go home."

The school year challenged my Australian resolve to enjoy life outside of the school environment. Long days drained my energy and immune system. Summer break was a welcome relief.

A Year Later, Summer 1997

"Good morning or, more accurately, good afternoon," my husband mocked.

"What time is it?" Absent-mindedly, I pulled an oversized dictionary from the bookshelf.

"Eleven-thirty. What are you doing?"

"I heard the words *a don a me* repeat in a dream." The massive book fell open to the French language section. "Didn't realize the dictionary had language sections."

"What do the words mean?"

"Hmmm, *don à moi*. 'A gift to me,' according to a French translation. Maybe we'll win the lottery."

* * *

Laurie's sister, Regina, phoned, "Hi cousin, Mom and I miss you. Any chance you could come for a visit?"

"Is tomorrow too soon?"

"Great, Mom will have your room ready. I'll call Laurie. Maybe she'll join us."

Anticipation started to build when I exited the freeway in the quaint beach town of San Clemente. Family gatherings, small or large, always generate feelings of joy, trust, and love.

Aunt Patti and I shared a close relationship. Her eyes glowed and radiated with an inner light. She appeared younger than her age. Her grace, insightful wisdom, spunk, and stories always inspired me.

My aunt and Regina greeted me at the door with smiles and warm hugs. After twenty minutes of cheerful exchanges of family pleasantries, our excitement took a breath.

Regina's mood turned serious. "Are you okay?"

"Been tired but feel great now," I responded.

Her pensive stare caused my face to flush as I broke eye contact.

"How about a quick stroll on the beach? You had a long drive. The fresh ocean air will do us both good. Mom won't mind."

Regina smiled at her mother. "Cocktails when we return?"

"Sure, honey." My aunt's eyebrows lifted. The tilt of her head showed confusion at the sudden change of plans, but her smile didn't waver.

My cousin and I stood quietly at the water's edge and watched gentle waves kiss the sand. They deposited an imprint of change and then retreated to the vast Pacific Ocean.

Regina broke the sea's hypnotic spell. She turned and focused on the necklace.

"What's that thing around your neck?"

"The necklace I bought in Australia. Don't you like it?"

"No!"

"Why?" I asked, stunned by her tone.

"It doesn't belong on you. There's something about it. I don't like it!" After a long pause, she asked, "Was it a consignment piece or preowned?"

I responded in a crossed-arm stance. "Yes. Why would that make a difference?"

"Tell me why you bought it."

I recounted the story for her.

Regina said with a slow, disbelieving shake of her head, "Can't understand why you'd even think about buying a necklace that's uncomfortable. How often do you wear it?"

"Nearly every day." I wanted to end this conversation, so I added, "It's getting late. Let's go back to your mom's."

The smell of Chinese food and the sound of laughter cleared the seriousness of the last two hours. "Now it's time for fun." Regina and I giggled in unison. We followed the trail of merriment to the living area of my aunt's home.

Laurie greeted her sister and me with a kiss on the cheek. "About time. We started without you."

"A scotch for Maureen and a vodka for me. Thanks, Tom," Regina said with a smile to her husband.

After dinner, Regina asked, "Tom, have you noticed Maureen's necklace?"

"Yes. Maureen, would you mind if I looked at it closer?"

I slipped the jewelry piece over my neck and handed it to him. "What's your opinion?" A minute later, he disappeared into the kitchen.

"Gina, come in here." Tom's tone sounded urgent.

Their hushed whispers piqued our curiosity. Laurie and I followed my aunt into the kitchen.

Regina backed away from the counter as she stared in shock. Her husband stood frozen. He glared at the object in front of him.

"Tom also sensed something negative before he dropped the necklace in a glass of salt water to cleanse the energy. The chain twisted and coiled up. Then hissed. The movement and noise haven't stopped."

Aunt Patti backed out of the room and rushed upstairs. Moments later, she returned, clutching something close to her heart.

"Get away from that, that thing!" she yelled.

"Regina, please put these on Maureen." She dangled a thin golden chain from one hand and cupped a small gold cross in the other.

"These belonged to Grandma. I don't like what just happened."

My aunt and I skipped our evening tea routine after everyone left. We both yearned for sleep.

Exhausted but unable to close my eyes, one thought reverberated through my mind. *Dispose of the necklace.* Tom and Laurie both volunteered to remove it from the house, but I told them that the responsibility belonged to me.

I heard my aunt's heavy breathing in the next room and crept downstairs. I went into the kitchen and picked up the paper bag where Tom had dumped the chain. I left by the side door. Hopefully, the salt water had eliminated the stone's possessed element or whatever it carried. I held the bag as if it contained a bomb that could explode at any minute and walked toward the trash bin outside the complex.

Early the next morning, I joined my aunt for coffee. She took a long, deep breath. "Honey, I can't find the sack." Her unfocused stare and shaky voice betrayed her calm demeanor.

"I needed to get the energy of that necklace away from us and out of your house. On my way to the trash bin, the contents squirmed and jerked. The bag became heavier and heavier. Unable to hold it any longer, I dropped it into the bushes, just steps from the trash container."

My aunt's complexion turned pale as she slipped down into the chair. A heavy sensation filled the room that triggered apprehension and mental exhaustion.

"Want to join me for fresh air? A walk to the park will clear our thoughts."

"You remember the way?"

I nodded.

"Don't get lost." My aunt smiled to lighten the mood.

"It's beautiful, isn't it?" A voice broke my trance. I noticed the ocean below me for the first time.

Startled, I turned in the direction of the voice and answered, "Yes, it is." A tall, well-dressed gentleman stood a few feet directly behind me in an open-leg stance. A dog sat at his side.

Now, with full awareness, I realized I had stopped about eight feet from the edge of a bluff that overlooked railroad tracks and the beach. I spun to speak to the man, but he was gone. Never heard or saw him leave.

Aunt Patti greeted me with a big bear hug. "Enjoy your walk?"

Confused and unable to explain the recent event to my aunt or myself, I answered, "Yes."

We rarely mentioned the unusual events of that visit. Ten years after the incident, Aunt Patti made a startling revelation.

"I've kept something to myself because I didn't know what to make of it. The incident frightened me, and I didn't want to worry you."

A shiver raced up my spine.

"Maureen, when you left for your walk, the day after the chain horror, I washed the glasses from the previous night. One of the crystal glasses jumped out of my hand and crashed into the sink. It shattered. This never happened before. A glass or two may have slipped from my hands, but not *jumped*."

Regina released a deep sigh. "Did you ever tell Mom about your walk?"

"No." I looked at my aunt.

"Now might be the right time."

My Questions and Lessons with the Australian Necklace

Daily occurrences impact our lives while we venture into uncharted territory each day. Reflections from past events guide our free will to either repeat a pattern or make a change. Years later, I realized events during the Australian trip had forewarned me of dangers when discernment trails behind actions.

A book, *The Secret,* by Rhonda Byrne revolutionized the law of attraction theory. Simply stated, like attracts like. Energy is the basis of everything. Our thoughts, beliefs, and emotions impact our surroundings and predict the present moment.

What force did I pick up when I opened to unknown realms of dimensions and asked Mother to come into my life? My energy at the time entertained defeat, fear, and desperation. The hasty decision is similar to unlocking the door of my home for strangers and inviting them to join me.

Today, I know my vibration when I enter trance states of consciousness for channeling, healing, and mediumship. I ask for Divine protection and remain in a state of joy, wonderment, trust, and love.

I still question the negativity associated with the necklace. Was it possessed, or did it carry an undesirable imprint from the previous owner? I've learned that personal objects like rings, watches, or necklaces hold the impression of the owner's magnetic energy field. The more a person wears the object, the stronger their signature mark is on the object. The chain and deep red-black stone I purchased at the metaphysical shop held the previous owner or owners' imprint. I'll never know what events occurred in the person's life that attached to the stone and medal. It didn't resonate with my energy.

Now I'm cautious about wearing jewelry that belonged to another person, including relatives. I won't wear it if it doesn't feel right or make me happy. It's the same for people and places, not everyone or every location fits my comfort zone.

Oddities Associated with the Australian Necklace

- Laurie's curiosity with the necklace sent her back the next day to retrieve the object from the bushes. She took it to a woman who dealt with the supernatural. Ms. A. sensed the deep red-black gemstone was old and held the spirit of a powerful Australian ancestor. The woman also commented that the energy felt too intense to wear for any length of time.
- A red spot surfaced on my chest bone where the stone had laid for a year. Three months later, the doctor diagnosed the lesion as skin cancer.

- The residual effects from the stone's energy lasted for weeks after I removed it from my neck. Every time I stepped into a religious store to purchase a cross, a feeling of suffocation and nausea assaulted me. Determined to release the necklace's power and energy, I sensed that holy water and prayer may be the answer.

- I located a Catholic Church in a town twenty miles from where I lived. With an acute sense of purpose, I carried two half-gallons of bottled water to the rectory entrance for a blessing and pushed the doorbell. When the priest opened the door, my calm demeanor changed to a high-pitched blabber as I pleaded for holy water due to an unknown force in my life. The man's eyes widened as he stepped back and slammed the door. Stunned, tears of frustration pooled in my eyes. The fear of defeat bubbled in every cell and instigated an adrenaline rush. I pounded on the door. The priest reluctantly emerged, spoke a few words as he made the sign of the cross over the bottles of water, and retreated into the rectory.

Gradually my life and emotions returned to normal after more than a year of turmoil. Since that time, I've always worn a cross. I feel it's my form of protection. More importantly, it serves as a reminder of my vulnerability and strength against unknown and unseen forces.

Many times, I've questioned the lessons that surrounded the Australian necklace. Did this object symbolize the power of shadows that dominated my life?

Seventeen years later, I received a message from an Australian actor, Daniel, who brought meaning to these dark forces that ransacked my life.

Questions to Ponder

Describe memories you want to bury or forget.

How do you cope with the effects of past hurts? What are the triggers or patterns?

What story do you tell yourself about your past or hurtful memories?

What can you do now to create a different version of your story to find peace or joy? What beliefs need to change?

Describe your life, at this present moment, with five words.

Chapter 5
"Lost Innocence, the Joker Laughs"

T he next interdimensional communication reveals the power of thoughts, actions, and addictions. I changed the identity of a well-known actor to the fictitious name of Daniel. The spirit's words remain exactly as I heard them. I share the research information that surrounded the entertainer's life to support and validate Daniel's message from the afterlife.

October 15, 2013

The name *Daniel* ascended in volume and strength within my mind as I struggled to decipher and grapple with dark phrases freshly scribbled in my journal from an early morning download. I knew little about this actor. Why would I hear his name and these daunting words? Uneasiness increased. I tossed the journal in the bottom drawer of my nightstand.

A month earlier, a new discipline called Human Design had seized my interest and monopolized my spare time. The combination of Western astrology, quantum physics, Kabbalah, and I Ching intrigued me. Based on the date, time, and place of my birth, I received valuable insight into my birth blueprint, ancestral influences, challenges, and strengths.

The topic of suicide and the devastating effects left on the lives of the survivors lingered in the forefront of my mind. I began to wonder if patterns found in Human Design charts of family members could flag inherited weaknesses for self-harm, addictions, or potential tragedies.

Days later, I delved deeper into Human Design concepts on the internet. Daniel's chart suddenly appeared on my computer screen. His name wasn't on the site I visited nor in my thoughts. The incident seemed strange.

I don't believe in coincidences as random. When they happen, I look for a reason. Curiosity triggers an internet search for answers or clues. In this case, I put Daniel's name in the search engine. Familiar words from the recent spirit download echoed in my mind as I probed into the actor's public appeal, movies, and commitment to the entertainment industry.

The following week a friend handed me a book titled *Messengers of Light: The Angels' Guide to Spiritual Growth* by Terry Lynn Taylor. This didn't surprise me. We discussed spiritual topics and divine timing many times. When I opened the book later that afternoon, the pages fell open to Chapter 31, "Cosmic Jokers: Archetypes of Evil." An eerie correlation between the spirit's transmitted phrases, Daniel's life, and cosmic jokers caused my chest to tighten.

I began to understand why I received the book. The author, Terry Lynn Taylor, shared information about the various angels that are available to assist us. She also included a chapter to discuss the constant battle between dark and light entities in our lives. Taylor explained that cosmic jokers represent evil that preys on negativity. They're creative and play with the minds and egos of humans under the influence or deprived of sleep.

I believe Daniel's spirit influenced the book exchange with my friend, not for the obvious reason (to expand my awareness of angels), but to provide context for his interdimensional communication. In Taylor's book and within the interdimensional communication, the joker represents a malignant force that feeds on obsessions, fears, and addictions.

"The Joker Took Over the Joke of Time"

October 5, 2013, 4:21 AM

A low-frequency hum interrupted my dream state. A sleepy glance at the clock: 4:21 a.m. Uneasiness washed over me as the glow from the digital numbers intensified. Words, heard in my mind, replaced the vibrational buzzing sound in my left ear. I grabbed the pen and notebook from my nightstand and recorded the incoming words.

The pain takes its toll on the mind and body
There are no more rational thoughts, just the decay of the mind
We become the joker of our reality
Peace comes at the expense of our existence
We now feel the sorrow of the fuel that fed us
How can we change and help others?
Only through the quickening of the mind
It is a lost reality
Brief, but it ends up a lifetime
Mine is the story of an escaped reality
Numbness wiped out the pain of daily existence
Insane? Maybe
The joker took over the joke of time
If only for a moment, light came
And maybe, just maybe
A glimmer of hope
Lost innocence, the joker laughs
The joker of life and darkness lives in the bottle of solitude
The bottle of lost hope and dreams
He lives in the needle, the final peace and serenity
He lives in the mind that succumbs to the false hope of peace,
helplessness, and faded dreams
The realm of darkness swallows the remnants of life
Tears are shed
The door closes

The light of hope diminishes
Ashes remain
Swallows fly home to nest and start again
Maybe next time there's hope
The perfect storm brews
The body of life prepares

The ominous phrases created a barricade in my mind and clouded the intent of the message during my first few readings. Confused and alarmed, I questioned if I wanted to decipher this download. The more I learned about Daniel's life and career, the more his spirit words became clear and opened my heart to reveal a message Daniel couldn't deliver in life or on the screen.

Daniel's Life Events that Support the Spirit Message

Daniel relayed strong messages and convictions through his movies. Determined to deliver performances that would impact audiences, he lived, studied, and morphed into the persona of the individual he portrayed. Perseverance and commitment fueled his passion as an artist. Psychological theories, neuroscience, and some spiritual teachings describe how our thoughts and actions manifest without conscious effort. I wondered if the roles Daniel portrayed on screen distorted his personal reality.

While he worked on his last few films, the actor's exhausted body and mental chatter triggered sleepless nights. Prescription drugs offered relief. Words within the spirit communication validated this. The spirit explains it in this manner: "Lost innocence, the joker laughs."

Through Daniel's performances, he created awareness about multiple aspects that intersect daily life today. I believe Daniel's soul continues this mission from the other side. The spirit communication suggests we appreciate the light and love around us, make changes if necessary, and understand our unique power and the gift of time before our life ends.

The spirit presents a question in the download: "How can souls in the afterlife change and help others (the living)? Through the quickening of the mind," the spirit informs us. The quickening of the mind refers to a shift in how we view things. What we once considered weird, taboo, or defying logic now has validity is more accepted, and has shifted to deeper exploration and scientific research. Communication with the departed and channeling are two examples of this phenomenon.

The phrase "quickening of the mind" exhibited profound implications in my life. For the past thirteen years, my point of view had shifted as I acknowledged beliefs contrary to Catholic dogmas. The words I share in this book would not exist if I hadn't surrendered to the path that my heart and several synchronicities led me to take.

From my experiences, the intelligence of the spirit world is mind-bending. It's not restricted by an ego, brain, time, or space. Unlimited knowing becomes possible when we remove our human blinders and allow filters to dissolve.

I didn't realize the full extent of the expression, "quickening of the mind," until my edits of this chapter in 2022.

After a late night of rewrites on Daniel's spirit transmission, I awakened to the repetition of the words, "quickening of the mind." The weight of this chorus buried all other thoughts.

The depth of these words escaped my understanding. *What did I miss?* I decided a walk in nature might clear my mind. As I listened to a guided meditation on YouTube, I asked Daniel's spirit for clarification of the spirit words.

Thirty minutes later I returned home, placed my keys and phone on the dining room table, and went into the kitchen to make lunch. When I checked the phone, my mind froze. The last session I had listened to on a meditation site lit up and indicated I had written a comment one second earlier on the site.

How could this be possible? I hadn't touched my phone within the last half hour and definitely didn't leave the comment, "Thank you (happy face emoji) Thank you (happy face emoji) Thank you (happy face emoji) I am happy (happy face emoji) Happy Birthday (happy face emoji) Thank you (happy face emoji)."

Unable to think in a coherent manner, I quickly deleted the remark. I didn't want my name associated with the strange remark left on a public meditation site.

Had I received a message from another realm on my phone? The question in my mind bellowed: *Who? My grandfather? His birthday would have been the next day. I've seen and experienced Granddad's spirit over the last fifty years.* It seemed a far stretch of the imagination to accept that a man born in the late 1800s would use technology and happy face emojis for his birthday reminder.

An hour later, the familiar atmospheric pressure change penetrated my left ear. The word *Daniel* pierced my thoughts. On impulse, I searched for the actor's name on the internet. Within minutes I discovered two clues that supported the nonsensical comment left on my phone. Daniel's birthday was in four days, and it also answered a question from one of his friends during a recent interview, "I wonder if Daniel is okay?"

If I struggled with what just materialized, wouldn't readers? The hardest part of this surreal incident was to let go of preconceived ideas, silence my ego and logic, and accept the present moment.

I believe this soul used the technology of a laptop and iPhone to redirect my attention to transmit his identity and messages. The strong bond of love and oneness across all dimensions through universal consciousness provides answers to questions held within the imagination. The quickening of the mind, or expansion of thought, opens our lives to limitless possibilities.

Daniel's Spirit Messages to the Living

Time, as we know it, passes quickly, much like life. Take back your power and innocence. Stay in control of your body, mind, and spirit.

Change occurs when we allow the doors of our reality to open and reveal new insights and possibilities. Shadows are dark areas of our lives. Secret obsessions and addictions assault the essence of life and joy. They resemble a predator that stalks, seduces, and controls its victim.

- *Dark and negative thoughts thrive in a bottle of alcohol or hide behind the mellowness of drugs.*
- *Compulsive or addictive behaviors lower self-worthiness.*
- *An escape from reality destroys the present moment and leads to lost tomorrows.*

Refuse to place your mind or consciousness in a safety deposit box that rarely opens. Turn the key to your imagination and experience new insights and possibilities. Expand the mind:

- *Observe and listen without judgment.*
- *Stay in the present moment.*
- *Be open to new ideas.*
- *Allow old and preconceived beliefs to take a timeout for a while. Free your ideas and thoughts.*

Appreciate the people in your life. Departed souls tell us, "I didn't see the love and support of others until I transitioned."

I feel the last two phrases in Daniel's spirit communication provide a peek into the possibility of reincarnation: After the spirit returns home, hope renews, a fresh script is written, and, just maybe, life begins again.

Man's mind, stretched to a new idea,
never goes back to its original dimension.
Oliver Wendell Holmes

The Correlation between Daniel's Spirit Message and the Shadows that Dominated My Life

The wisdom behind the spirit words illuminated aspects of my life that I ignored or refused to acknowledge. My demons resided in the memories of childhood. They fed my insecurities through an obsession with school, work, exercise, and perfectionism and nurtured a need for approval and acceptance. A state of victimhood and the inability or refusal to forgive blocked healing and made it impossible for me to move forward. Alcohol camouflaged emotions and time. Awareness and a desire for change instigated a chance to reclaim my life and the present moment.

"We become the joker of our reality."

The arms of insecurities and addictions that surround us execute a false sense of safety. They become sown into our daily existence. "If only for a moment, the light came and maybe, just maybe, there would be a glimmer of hope."

"Relax, it's okay," says the spider to the fly. "I
won't hurt you.
The web of ambush tightens. The freedom of flight
ends."
Mary Howitt

The strongest principle of growth lies in human choice.
George Eliot

Strategies to Eliminate an Addiction or Unwanted Habit:

- Awareness of a problem.
- Know why you want to change.
- Seek support from family, friends, support groups, or professionals.
- Identify and understand triggers so you can recognize them.
- Replace an unwanted habit with a positive activity.
- Remove temptations and avoid situations or people that trigger unwanted behavior.
- Take one step at a time for change.
- Practice patience, perseverance, and a desire to change.
- Seek and ask for God's help.
- Relapses are part of the journey. Learn to readjust your mindset. Don't give up!
- Celebrate small and big milestones along your path to personal freedom.

Questions to Ponder

Shadows steal our self-worth, the joy of life, and compassion. They become habits.

Examples of shadows: Drug or alcohol addictions, smoking, pornography, overeating, eating disorders, excessive shopping and spending, excessive social media use, workaholism, hoarding, excessive gaming, control issues, explosive anger, or anything that becomes excessive.

Do you have shadows that you hide behind or keep from others? Why?

What or who triggers them?

Do shadows/addictions affect your values, mood, or quality of life with yourself or others?

Would you want to change a habit or take control over an aspect of your life?

What memories from the past instigate fear or insecurities?

What behaviors rob minutes or hours of your day?

Do these subtract from the life you want?

What habits cause friction with family or friends?

Has an addiction gravitated to a habit or crutch to survive or get through the day? How and why?

Do you have the motivation or purpose to regain control?

What would your perfect day look like to get the most out of this life?

If I had more time each day, I'd ...

If I had an extra hour in my day, I'd ...

Awareness is the first step to change. What would the next step involve for change in your life?

How would this change boost your self-image and quality of life?

Does the quote from Daniel's download apply to you, "Lost innocence, the joker laughs"?

Do any words from Daniel's story resonate with you? Why?

Chapter 6

A Psychic Boot Camp

Self-doubt became a constant companion after my first spirit message in 2013. I questioned what caused this new reality: *Is it really souls on the other side or a colorful imagination?* Either way, I needed answers. I booked a flight to England. Arthur Findlay College, a renowned school of psychic and mediumship development, would either confirm or negate whether I exhibited paranormal capabilities or abnormal behavior.

Earlier in my exploration into the afterlife, a group leader shared about her training at Arthur Findlay College in England. She uncovered her innate mediumship abilities and confidence to explore intangible occurrences. This world-renowned facility, in the study of spiritualism and psychic sciences, has tutored many mediums and healers over the years.

Thoughts of plane travel over twelve hours and 5,400 miles for paranormal classes didn't interest me at the time. A fifteen-mile trip to Ojai, California, at twenty dollars per class was the perfect alternative.

The background noise of my religion, along with new abilities to hear words and vibrational tones, weaved a cloak of uncertainty and guilt. Synchronicities, dreams, and automatic writing became more persistent and focused over the next eight months.

Insecurities about travel to a foreign country slid into the back seat. A thirst for explanations took the wheel. Having been diagnosed with dyslexia in college and having a poor sense of direction caused family and friends to question my mental judgment when I announced plans to travel to England, alone and past the old age of sixty-five.

My first visit to Arthur Findlay College morphed into a Harry Potter ride through Disneyland. I discovered the magic of surrender and trust while my soul soared into a dreamlike world of unfamiliar wonderment.

A six-day stay at the magnificent sprawling English estate, rebuilt in 1871, made the term *psychic boot camp* sprout legs. I hobbled through classrooms of the supernatural, which turned up the volume of my six senses.

Long days at Arthur Findlay started with breakfast at 8:00 a.m., followed by mediumship and psychic development classes from 9:30 a.m. to 9:00 p.m. Small groups of twelve students with one tutor provided the confidence to explore hidden abilities in a supportive and nonjudgmental environment. Vulnerabilities and fears were gangsters that needed to be gunned down for forward movement in the foreign land of the paranormal.

Thirty-six acres of sprawling landscaped grounds provided a perfect retreat into the world of nature and the mystical realms. I realized why this college held students in a hypnotic trance of addiction. It's a playground for the spirit and soul.

The fluidity of my transformation into the world of mediumship and channeling transpired in a seamless manner. Two spirits who passed by suicide and another from substance abuse delivered messages of healing through me. These, along with spirit messages prior to this trip, instigated a special bond of love and compassion with victims of this type of death. It opened a gift that materialized on the doorstep of my retirement.

I witnessed many wondrous effects of blending the Earthly and non-Earthly realms at Arthur Findlay College. Through workshops, evidential mediumship readings, spiritual healings, and fellow students' interactions with the afterlife, logic disappeared. Surrender to inner knowing and trust emerged.

Chapter 7
A Teenage Spirit:
"Will I Be Missed? Maybe Not."

The week prior to Lenny's interdimensional communication, the media reported two unrelated suicides. Both victims were teenagers. This type of death had started to infiltrate the news at an alarming frequency. As a teacher and principal, I had witnessed middle school students' vulnerability, sensitivity, and innocence between the ages of twelve and fifteen. A need for acceptance plays a key role in their development, especially during the teen years.

The surge in death by suicide among our youth haunted me. What thorns pierced these young hearts, numbed their feelings, and stole their desire to live?

My recent study of Human Design triggered questions about the depth of this discipline. Could similarities in ancestral or birth traits of suicide victims reveal red flags for a disposition to self-harm or depression?

My prayers begged for the stamina to bypass emotions and bring light to this heart-wrenching subject. Over the next month, I printed a Human Design graph and data on seventeen recent suicides with an age range from twelve to twenty-one. I methodically placed each case in a folder, unread. Empathy for each innocent young person and their grieving family paralyzed my emotions. This prevented further investigation.

It took three weeks to gather the courage to review and compare all the collected information placed in the file. Individual details of each death exposed gut-twisting narratives. Various scenes unfolded in my mind's eye. The consequences of intimidation, bullying, and jealousy painted scenes of fear, worthlessness, and lost hope. Mentally I pleaded to ease the sensations that ravaged every cell in my body.

Within moments, a familiar energy tugged at my senses. A high-toned buzzing in my left ear initiated a lightheadedness. Thoughts vanished. My mind surrendered to the stillness that invaded my surroundings. Instinctively I understood a spirit wanted acknowledgment. The name *Lenny* repeated in my mind. The energy felt like a young person around the age of thirteen. With pen and journal in hand, words methodically covered the paper as I drifted into a semi-conscious state of trance.

Lenny's Channel, August 12, 2014, 4:33 p.m.

My body ached when I telepathically heard the words and felt the emotions of many souls. One spirit stepped forward to speak:

"Floods of emotions come crashing through the barriers. The wound opens and the pain lays bare."
I tried to make it go away
The voices wouldn't stop
It isn't okay, not anymore
It won't stop.
Silent giggles and whispers are heard
Teachers look the other way.
"Just stay out of the way," I say.
They follow and ridicule
Why me? I'm not to blame
I don't want to play their game.
I'll show them, I'll go away
I'll disappear

Will I be missed?
Maybe not
They'll be sorry.
I see their false tears now
But wait, they look real.
Now I'm safe
But can't go back.
Mom cries so much.
I'm sorry, hear my voice, I'm near
See me
Feel me
I want to hug and play
I'm sorry
I is not the same.
Teach them to love, not fight
Teach them the value of their lives
Teach them they are perfect
Don't need to please
Teach them to love.
I'm sorry.

Tears blurred my vision when the transmission ceased. I sat motionless. Nothingness dissolved the present reality. When the ability to form thoughts returned, I read the spirit communication.

Anguish and sorrow rippled through the spirit words. Lenny's spirit message exposed the intimate feelings of an adolescent harassed by others. Powerlessness and defeat surfaced. Only 20 to 30 percent of those bullied confide in their parents or teachers. A cracked mirror of self-respect shatters as loneliness increases.

I feel that the statement, *I want to come back to play*, reveals the view of a young person who didn't understand the consequences of his last action on Earth. Lenny needed the taunting from his peers to stop. In his mind, if he made the bullies sorry for their actions, the harassment might end. Now, the departed soul observes and feels the grief and pain of the family and friends he left behind.

The statement, "I is not the same" caused trepidation as I reread the line many times. *Did I misinterpret or write down the wrong word from the spirit? Possible.* For the purity of all my channeled communications, I've duplicated the exact expressions heard in meditation or semi-trance states of consciousness. To me, the spirit stated he, Lenny, changed when his soul transitioned into the next realm. Insight from a life review revealed the importance of self-respect, self-acceptance, and boundaries. Individuals struggle with these skills daily.

A limited number of people witness bullying and power games at school, but it spreads like fire through social media. It turns into a sport played by some and observed by many. A person's lack of confidence often feeds the appetite of a bully. The need to humiliate or destroy another's reputation gives them power. Silence from the spectators fuels their hunger. This spirit message opens the vault to our youth's emotional and social instability. In this case, neither the victim nor the aggressor understood the full impact of their actions.

The last five lines highlight the simplicity and importance of the spirit's message: "Teach individuals to value their lives."

Spirit Wisdom from a Young Soul

- *Life is fragile, especially during times of stress and anxiety.*

- *I feel sorry for the grief I caused so many.*

- *Teach individuals to value their lives.*

- *Teach about the quality of uniqueness within each person.*

- *Teach the importance of self-respect and boundaries for another's inappropriate behavior.*

- *Remind the youth they are not alone and to ask for help, even if it's hard.*

- *A young person's problems matter. Take them seriously.*

- *Suicide is a final act; it can't be undone.*

- *Mom, trust I'm always near.*

Tragically, suicide is the second leading cause of death for people ages ten to fourteen and twenty-five to thirty-four. It's the third leading cause of death among individuals ages fifteen to twenty-four and the fourth leading cause of death among individuals thirty-five to forty-four.[2]

Over 3,069 of our youth in grades nine to twelve attempt suicide each day. The numbers are higher among seventh- and eighth-grade students.[3]

---

[2] 2022 Centers for Disease Control and Prevention (CDC), Web-based Statistics Query and Reporting System.
[3] 2019 Data from the Youth Risk Behavior Surveillance System of the CDC.

It's shown that certain factors put individuals at higher risk for suicidal thoughts and actions:

- Those who identify as lesbian, gay, bisexual, transgender, or questioning.
- Family history of suicide.
- History of physical, mental, or sexual abuse.
- Drug or alcohol use.
- Stressful life events.
- Feelings of social isolation.
- Bullying.

The need for guidance and support for a child doesn't stop in the teen years. These young adults need your watchful eye as they learn to feel comfortable with independence and adulthood. Your presence and confidence in them as individuals are more important than ever in this changing world.

Listen more. Show you care and are interested in their life.

- A young person's stress is real, not always a hormonal problem. Ask and listen.
- Set clear and concise boundaries and be consistent with the consequences. Explain why the rules are important.
- Discipline with love, respect, and genuine concern. Avoid anger.
- Words and actions hold a lot of power and influence. Make them kind and meaningful to the development of your child.
- Allow your child the freedom to make age-appropriate decisions and learn from their actions. They're building the foundation for adulthood.
- Watch for changes in your teen's behavior, appearance, or attitude about school or friends, academic performance, and internet usage. It's not the same world you knew at their age.
- Four out of five individuals with thoughts of suicide give a sign of their intentions through words or behavior. Be aware and listen.

- Monitor the use of social media, apps, and software. Identify sites that put your child in danger. Show an interest in their postings and online gaming activities.
- Talk with your teen about alcohol, drugs, stress levels, and sex. Don't shy away from the conversation where over 6,000 parents risk losing their children in a single day from a death by suicide.

Don't worry that children never listen to you;
worry that they are always watching you.
Robert Fulghum

Questions to Ponder

Have you asked your teenager about school, their friends, who they sit with during lunch or on the bus, who they hang around with during recess or breaks, and what they're doing during this time? How do they feel about what is happening at school? Watch for signs of isolation, uneasiness, inconsistent responses, or fear.

Ask about social media accounts or contacts they make online. Do they notice any rude or bullying comments about a friend?

Have you discussed the subject of bullying with your child or what can be done if they witness bullying with others?

Have you ever been bullied in the past? How did you react? How would you respond to bullying today in your life?

What advice would you give a young person or adult who allows bullying to interfere with their happiness?

Chapter 8
My March Down the Dark Corridor
—Part I

Past hurts, especially from people we love, are difficult to forget or release. They prey on the subconscious, berate the self-image, and weave a disheartened personal tale. The narrative loses its sting when thoughts shift to view the injustices from a nonjudgmental perspective. Often the person who inflicted the hurtful behavior also coexists as a victim of circumstance.

The act of forgiving breaks the bond of another's invisible grip. It frees the imprisonment of deep-rooted anger and emotions. Strength of character and perseverance lift the rock of pain to expose a glimmer of light. This initiates the freedom to grow and heal.

The thought of forgiving my mother seemed unimaginable. My retort to people and relatives who offered free, unwanted advice on the subject, "Why would I forgive her?" From early memory, Mother's constant alcoholic rages of verbal and mental abuse frightened me and my siblings.

My role as a child shifted into a maternal role at the age of ten when a baby sister arrived on the scene, followed by a brother eighteen months later. Dad's business kept him out of town most of the week. When he returned home, Mother's violent outbursts forced him to leave again. Eventually, Dad moved out of the house.

"Maureen, I'm divorcing your mom and need your help. If you testify in court and tell the judge what happens when I'm not in the house, there's a chance I may get custody of all of you."

I didn't understand the scope and damage of custody battles at thirteen but trusted my dad would make things better. He and I had a close father-daughter relationship or, as my stepmother described it, a platonic husband-wife relationship. I turned into his confidante and emotional comforter, which in turn made me feel needed, loved, and protected.

Mother discovered I broke the family code of silence and testified against her in court. Hurt and bitter, she released her wrath on me. When forced out of the house for days at a time, my sisters and brother became her target.

Fifteen months after the court episode, Dad called. "The divorce is final. Can we meet in an hour? Need to talk about something." I met him in our usual spot around the corner from the house.

Dad looked tired and greeted me with a faint smile and kiss on the cheek. Cigarette smoke smothered the fresh air as it tried to enter through partially closed windows. He took a deep breath. "You know Elizabeth and I have been dating for a while. Since the divorce is finalized, we've decided to get married."

I forced a smile. "Will we be living with you and Elizabeth?"

"She isn't comfortable raising four extra children along with her daughter. Elizabeth agreed that Sheila and Dennis could live with us after our marriage."

"Do Carol and I have to stay with Mommy?"

Dad's eyes watered as he broke eye contact. "I can't let that happen. You've missed too much school. Do you remember Clif and Anne? You met them a month ago."

"The older couple from Bakersfield?"

"I've known them for years. They never had children of their own and offered to take good care of you and Carol. They're excited about it." Dad paused to check my reaction. "The only other option is boarding school."

My emotions froze. Nothing seemed real.

"When would we go to Bakersfield?"

"Friday."

"But it's Christmas in one week!"

"You'll know the neighborhood and area before school resumes in January. To avoid a scene from your mother, I'll meet you here Friday morning. She'll think both of you left for school. Pack a suitcase and leave it at the side of the house Thursday night."

Through choked tears, I yelled, "What about Sheila and Dennis? They can't stay at the house without us!"

"They'll be with your grandmother for a few weeks until I get everything settled with your mother and the house."

Mother began her slippery downhill road to alcoholism in her teen years. Her dependency on liquor, or any form of alcohol, ruled her life. When she couldn't get wine or vodka the last few years of her life, she consumed fingernail polish remover. Mother died in the hospital at the age of forty-six, after she drank her favorite perfume.

I'm not sure when my state of detachment turned into a means of survival. As happens with many victims of abuse, suppressed emotions hide behind a mask that dons a smile.

The nightmare of my arrest, while driving under the influence of alcohol, changed my life. Six months of weekly, mandated DUI classes focused on substance abuse and its consequences. I listened to members of our group share stories about their drug of choice. Three-fourths of the people arrested in this group used pills, drugs, and/or alcohol to escape physical or emotional pain and life.

The third week of DUI classes released a volcano of blocked memories. Voices and images of the past emerged from the walls as I completed the homework assignment: Describe the pink elephant in the room. They held one thing in common: Mother's alcoholism.

Silent questions started to replace blame. *What caused Mother to wash away days, months, and years of her life with alcohol?* No one knows for sure.

We cannot start over, but we can begin now,
And make a new ending.
Zig Ziglar

Chapter 9

Tommy: "The Disease of Pain"

Forgiveness remains a difficult choice for people. A victim who relives the past casts tall shadows that swallow reality, rehash pain, and fling blame. The sting of hurt remains active. Actions and thoughts dictate a person's happiness.

A well-known musician, now in the afterlife, downloaded a personal message to the living through me. I changed the performer's identity to the fictitious name of Tommy. All the interdimensional words remain precisely as I received them. A preliminary search into the artist's life revealed a global admiration for Tommy's musical abilities, although his music and style remained unfamiliar to me until his spirit communication.

I waded through the download but failed to understand the intent of the unworldly visitation. I dug deeper into Tommy's life. Gradually, vitality infused breath into the spirit's words. Childhood memories haunted this artist throughout his lifetime. Tommy's spirit shares his story about the disease of emotional pain.

Tommy's Channel, January 11, 2015

A shiny globe of light spun in the southwest corner of my room during the predawn hours of January 11, 2015. The tighter I closed my eyes, the brighter the illumination. The name *Tommy* echoed in my mind. An energy of a spirit communicator rose to a crescendo and instigated an involuntary reflex to grab my pen and journal from the nightstand. Words spilled from the writing instrument onto the paper. Thoughts faded while I drifted into a light sleep state during the spirit-dictation process.

The band played forever
Girls flowed in and out with champagne glasses
Life is splendid— no money crashes
Diamonds, cars, and parade of parties
The sadness of the time left little to the imagination
When the crash hit, it took us to the streets
Penny for your thoughts
Darkness in every alley, snow and weed in every corner
We all fell down
Street of sleekness, no downers here
The bottom gets deeper, can't climb out
Lost dreams, the sadness eats from within
The bottle is always empty— just one more
The wives walk out, the party never stops
Broken promises, false hopes, doesn't matter anymore
Visions of yesteryear fade, drink some more
The bottle of hidden peace and surrender
Mishaps, mistakes, vanity takes over
Sadness around the corner
When will it stop
Window of hope fades into the darkness
I'm sorry, I'm sorry
The rain came down and won
Take us one by one, it is all the same
The window of hope closes
Whistles fade, lost dreams, love, and the blues
I'm sorry
Call to the monkeys before it is too late
Purple
The disease of pain destroys

Can't hide anymore
No more, no more
The light is greater than the darkness
But only thrives in the darkness of the mind
I'm sorry, just—I'm sorry
Lost identity destroys the soul.

After I concluded my research into the musician's life and interpreted the interdimensional communication, I asked Tommy's spirit to validate that he authored this message.

The following morning, I turned on the car radio. Instead of the anticipated local news station, an unfamiliar music station's DJ announced, "Tommy is the artist of the next track." This was the first time I recall hearing any of the artist's music on the radio. The title of the song indicated Tommy's spirit not only authored the transmitted words but also watched over the delivery of his message to the public.

Tommy's Life Events that Support the Spirit Transmission

"Broken promises and false hopes" colored Tommy's early years. His parents' heavy drinking triggered arguments and caused his mother to leave the house many times. The spirit reveals "the wives walk out."

Tommy's mother passed during his teen years. He and his younger brother were given shots of whiskey and told, "This is how men deal with grief and pain."

I believe the first four lines of the spirit communication describe Tommy's success at the height of his career.

Another validation Tommy's spirit authored this afterlife communication refers to a contentious war: "The sadness of the time left little to the imagination." This young musician, already a veteran at the time, vocalized strong opinions through a song that gained worldwide attention.

The spirit informs us about the easy access and availability of drugs sold on the street at that time. Is it any different today? As of April 13, 2023, The Centers for Disease Control and Prevention reports that ninety-one people die each day in the United States from an opioid overdose. Alcohol-related daily deaths in the United States, according to the CDC in 2023, are over 383. The statements in this download contain a stark warning to individuals: The crutches of drugs or alcohol enable, destroy, and kill. An overdose of these substances contributed to Tommy's early death.

Tommy's popularity and singing career gained global recognition, especially during his last four years. He toured the US with a famous band for awhile. Tommy's spirit's reference to the band may attempt to convey a message to one of the surviving members.

The last sentence in the spirit communication summarizes the essence of Tommy's short life: "Lost identity destroys the soul." Neither fame nor money could erase deep-rooted memories from the singer's past. Tommy's spirit warns the living to reclaim their identity, their life, and their individual power. Let go of the past because it contributes to "the disease of pain."

Tommy's Spirit Messages to the Living

- *Let go of pain from the past. It produces a darkness that bleeds into the mind, body, and ego.*

- *Drugs and alcohol create a distorted perception of reality.*

- *Addictions turn into bottomless pits, difficult to overcome.*

- *Living within the bubble of emotional sorrow leads to lost hope, dreams, and joy. It unleashes the disease of pain.*

- *Drug and alcohol-related deaths take people, one by one.*

- *Avoid the dangers of traveling down streets that lead nowhere except into murky alleys of your life.*

- *U-turns become difficult.*

- *"I'm sorry," echoed Tommy.*

Questions to Ponder

What memories influence your life now?

Do you have control over your life? Do you allow outside influences to dictate your emotions or behavior?

What boundaries have you set for the negative outside influences (people, situations, self-talk) in your life?

Do you allow negative remarks or behaviors to interfere with your self-worth?

Do you make excuses for another's unwanted behavior?

What situations or people impact your life? How or why?

Name three negative influences.

Name three positive influences.

What does the phrase "disease of pain" mean to you?

What remedies/actions would you share with a person to help them heal from the disease of pain?

What does the phrase "quality of life" mean to you?

Did anything resonate with you in Tommy's chapter? Why?

We can easily forgive a child who is afraid of the dark;
the real tragedy of life is when men are afraid of the light.
Plato

Chapter 10

A Spirit's Urgent Message

September 5, 2014

The power and tenacity of the spirit realm to deliver time-sensitive messages amazes me. Their communications do not rely on idle words; instead, all dimensional insights contain a gem of wisdom that must be opened, examined, assimilated, and shared.

Katie, a client of mine, asked me to meet with her mother, Gloria. Her mother's anxieties caused stress and friction in the mother-daughter relationship. Gloria felt that a relative had put a *curse* on her. Frustrated, Katie felt that I might bring awareness to the situation.

I didn't know anything about curses nor did I want to become involved in this type of situation. My intuition and heart overruled the option to say "No!"

Even though nervous, anxious, and unsure, I welcomed Katie and Gloria on the day of our scheduled meeting. The energy I picked up around the two women caught me off guard. It appeared light, not negative.

Our conversation uncovered other issues that probably triggered Gloria's chaos.

Toward the end of our time together, Gloria mentioned that her husband died by suicide after his doctor gave him an incurable diagnosis for his failing health. I told the wife, Gloria, and the man's stepdaughter, Katie, that souls channeled through me and provided insight into suicide, if they wished to discuss this type of death further.

In a low, sad voice, Katie asked me if I would channel her son's girlfriend. A year earlier, Ashley, age twenty-two, took her life. Gloria placed the paper with Ashley's name on the table. Ice raced through my veins.

Fifteen minutes after the ladies' departure, a spirit's voice invaded my mind. The words came fast. Deep sorrow seeped through me.

Tell him I loved him.
My demons, not important—not him—I loved him.
Life is hard.
Pain I couldn't release.
I'm sorry
Thank you for believing in me
Much to live for, I can see now
Ghost movie—I will always be with you.
Believe, please believe.
I see now why and what I left behind
Believe
I'm sorry—I love you
Please give him this message
He needs it now
Tears of joy and pain mixed together
Thank you my love
I'm so sorry
Please forgive me—always with you, my love
Thank you for believing
Pink champagne... so many bubbles of love.
Will be forever near—live, live, live now
Rejoice in my love that was yours
Live now as we would have lived
Live from the heart with joy—the joy we knew
PLEASE, PLEASE, PLEASE RELEASE THE PAIN

The underlying tone and urgency of this message left little room for doubt. Ashley's spirit needed me to deliver her message. I recalled the events that led to Ashley's channel and wondered how much power her spirit executed to arrange a meeting between her fiancé's mother, grandmother, and me. The way Ashley's name entered the conversation wasn't a coincidence.

The urgency of the spirit's words, "Please give him this message. He needs it now," persuaded me to contact Katie.

I soon understood the timeliness of the spirit's words for Katie's son. The heartache and despair when Ashley took her life sent Katie's son into his own suicide mission. He treaded the fragile line between life and death often. He blamed himself for Ashley's death. Grief dominated his thoughts and emotions.

Katie's son needed to understand he was not responsible for his girlfriend's suicide. Ashley's spirit words confirmed, it was "my demons." "Pain I couldn't release."

The message from his girlfriend's spirit helped the young man deal with his grief and loss. Ashley's spirit observed the consequences of her actions and the pain she'd caused the man who loved and wanted to marry her.

"Please release the pain," "I'm sorry," and "I loved you" echoed throughout Ashley's download.

Eighteen months after this incident, I spoke with Katie again. She shared words that filled my heart with appreciation for the timeliness of Ashley's message.

"Thank you so much for the message to my son. He knows now he's loved. With the words you passed on to him, he chose to move forward."

The greatest discovery of my generation is that a human being can alter his life by altering his attitude of mind.
William James

Questions to Ponder

Has grief following someone's death affected your physical, mental, or spiritual life?

Can you identify the pain? What steps would you take to move forward in your life?

Name three actions you can take to enhance the quality of your life.

Which of the three will be your first step toward change?

Did anything in Ashley's channel resonate with you?

*The secret to change is to focus all of your energy
not on fighting the old,
but on building the new.*
Socrates

Chapter 11
Little Blue Angel

In the next section, an entertainer's spirit conveyed a poignant message about the importance of self-respect. Daily challenges stripped joy, dignity, and love from her short Earthly existence. "Too many demands, too many highs, too little love" peppered the singer's life while she struggled with inner peace and acceptance.

This maverick artist defied music norms and electrified audiences with a tempestuous, charismatic stage presence. When the curtain came down, hollowness and voices from the past inhabited her lonely, loveless nights. Memories of high school bullying and rejections haunted her sensitive nature. Alcohol and drugs brought comfort.

I didn't follow this entertainer during her lifetime. Heartfelt admiration for the singer's depth, beauty, and soul unfolded after I researched her life and the significance of the interdimensional communication.

I changed the name of the spirit communicator to the fictional name of Helen. The spirit phrases were not altered; all words, except one, remain as I received them.

October 21, 2014

I'd completed the last errand on my to-do list. The day felt longer than usual. Autumn's seductiveness ushers in crisper weather, earlier sunsets, and comfy clothes and fosters a slower pace. *It must be the change of seasons*, I told myself.

The Bluetooth system flashed an incoming call within moments after I started the car for the drive home. I checked my cell for the identification of the caller, but the phone didn't display signs of a call. I turned off the ignition and powered off the mobile device. Within seconds, the incoming disturbance disappeared.

Adrenaline shot through my system. Thoughts raced back to September 9, 2014, the evening I channeled an unnerving message during a mediumship circle. A similar incident had occurred with my car.

A blurry recollection of an early morning visitation aroused my curiosity on the drive home. *Hmmm. I wonder if I recorded it.*

After entering the house, a journal entry confirmed that I *had* recorded a spirit communication during the early morning hours; a predawn transmission that I hadn't even remembered. I had no recollection of the visitation until my car and phone replicated the September 9th activity.

When I slip into a trance state, intuitively or deliberately, my mind travels between the conscious and unconscious, much like the sleep state. If the automatic writing process is initiated, sleep usually follows when the pen stops moving across the page. Memories fade unless something triggers the recall. This is not uncommon.

October 21, 2014, 5:05 AM

Noisy chatter dimmed the peacefulness of sleep in the predawn hours. Alertness increased. Alone in the room, I sensed an unseen presence. Immediately, I heard in my mind, "Please hear me."

"Who is this?" I fumbled for my notebook and pen on the side table.

"Helen."

The name triggered a flash of recognition. I replied telepathically, "Validation, please." Instantly, spirit-initiated communication started. My hand recorded the incoming words without effort or interference from my mind. Sleep followed.

Spirit message to me:

The music is loud, hear me
The pace is fast, don't shut me out
Birds flutter close to be heard
Yes, we watch, we cry, we were lost
You understand
Can hear the cries, the moans

Spirit message to all:

The voices are many
The whispers constant
The pasture is thick with fog
The night is lonely, the stars are many
Voices pierce my silence, can't stop
Stillness never comes without a price
Take the rose—smell the fragrance
It once satisfied the soul
The hunger of the soul searched for more
Temptation and pain took over
The valley stretched out over the horizon, deep into paradise
Paradise of lost dreams
So many fans, so many masks, alive at least
Then the curtain came down—the musky hollowness took over
I'm lost
I'm oh so sorry, talent taken for granted
"Little Blue Angel"
I sang my heart out—never enough
Too many demands, too many highs, too little love
Dark loves
Hidden secrets no one can know
Time marches on
The drummer is quick, the pace becomes its own
Down the street of nowhere

A rest was needed—find new hope
Tired—no more, not for a while
The rainbows will come back
The bird will sing again—but needs a rest
Time to learn and gather my wit
I'm sorry
I took the wrong course
Couldn't forgive and forget
It was my loss
Numbness becomes reality
No more please
Release me now
The light will follow the night
I'm sorry
The curse, the pain, the curtain came down
Soon I will be back
My voice will sing again
Please hear my cry of hope and faith
Believe you are the best
Know your heart
Feel the flow that keeps you abreast
Find a new song from the heart
Change the course
Follow my words
Lessons of love
Lessons of hope
Lessons of strength will endure
Please forgive
Hear the song of the blues
The soul can dance,
The voice will shout, "Live, my dear, with hope."
Forget lost dreams
Dance with joy
The time is short, but the night is long
Let go of darkness

Sing the joys of life
Much to understand.

Helen's Life Supported the Spirit Words

Helen's voice vibrated through the hearts of her fans when she performed. Their acceptance and love freed her inner passion. Songs unveiled raw beliefs about fears, love, and vulnerabilities that mirrored her own experiences and silent pain. This same openness infiltrated phrases of the spirit's transmission.

Emotional numbness, "dark love," and addictions quietly stole Helen's reality and soul. I believe this contributed to the singer's tiredness described in the download.

Helen's soul's plea, "Don't shut me out," and her message to me appear in the first two stanzas of the download. Her dynamic spirit personality and insistence to deliver a new song of hope and change to her audience continue to defy norms and conventions. Helen's spirit utilized channeling to convey her story of change in the afterlife.

I also believe Helen's spirit provided references to reincarnation: "Soon I will be back. The bird will sing again." The transmitted communication hints that her next visit to this dimension will incorporate lessons of love, joy, hope, and strength learned in the invisible world after her transition.

Forty-two Days Earlier, September 9, 2014

Mediumship development circles are an integral part of my week. Several mediums and I gather to explore and strengthen our paranormal skills while we relay and interpret messages from the spirit world. On September 9, 2014, I received an interdimensional communication during silent meditation that tugged at my heart and exposed the sender's vulnerabilities.

The pain grows, no more.
I tried, Mom—forgive me, please.
No more, no more, no more, no more.
The cries grow louder, please no more
Happy Birthday, Josh

Fear gripped my emotions. My oldest son's recent challenges and his birthday in two days caused my mind to swerve from reality. Did my subconscious add, *Happy Birthday*? Who telepathically transmitted these phrases? Desperate to understand, I searched the previous page of my journal for clues. The words I transcribed while in a state of trance read, "Tears of pain, release. Relief is coming. The experience is needed."

Panic replaced logic by the time the meeting ended. I needed to hear my son's voice.

The car's Bluetooth showed a received or outgoing call when I started the engine. No indication of a call registered on my cell phone. I turned off the engine and powered off the phone. Neither of these actions stopped the interference with the car's infotainment system. The hindrance disabled my phone, radio, and navigation system on the thirty-minute drive home. All car systems returned to normal after I shut off the engine in my driveway. The mobile phone never recorded a call.

This was the first time a situation with the navigation system occurred. More than a month later, the day I channeled Helen's message, October 21, 2014, the car's Bluetooth reacted in a similar manner.

I'm confident spirits manipulate electronics to get our attention. Helen's spirit validated that she delivered the message in meditation on September 9th and again forty-two days later, on October 21st. I believe her spirit energy disabled my navigation system, radio, and cell phone on both those days to confirm the connection between the two messages. My car's dealership couldn't find a malfunction or reproduce what happened with the car's Bluetooth on those two occasions.

Spirits' ability to seize my attention and tie both messages together testify to their boundless qualities and presence.

Helen's first passage on September 9th triggered panic within every cell of my body. Was I about to lose my son to a death by suicide?

The words on the preceding page of my journal, "Relief is coming. The experience is needed," didn't make sense at the time, and only heightened my confusion and powerlessness.

My son's words, "Mom, I'm okay. Stop worrying," brought relief, but that brief anguish left an emotional stain on my heart for all parents who lose a child, especially by suicide.

Another reason I believe Helen's spirit delivered both messages: The singer composed a birthday song for a fellow entertainer before she passed.

To me, the two downloads indicate her love and dedication to fans worldwide continues today. Helen's spirit relayed an important reminder: Only you can change your happiness and life.

Show performances nurtured the singer's thirst for acceptance, love, and personal identity. Helen never appreciated her influence, inner beauty, or self-worth. How many people today rely on their career or work to dictate their identification, story, and happiness?

Helen's Message to the Living

After years in the afterlife, Helen's spirit used three words to summarize concepts and circumstances that escape Earthly comprehension: (there is) "much to understand."

Wisdom from the Other Side:

Love begins in your heart, for yourself, then extends out to others.

Listen to your heart. Know what makes you happy. Follow this path.

Forgive and forget. "It was my loss."

Self-worthiness starts with self-respect. Happiness and inner peace follow.

Earthly life is short. Life after transition is long. Be aware of moments and days. They can't be replaced.

Delete self-judgment and negative comments from the past. Change your story.

Let go of darkness. Allow your light to shine. Believe in you.

You're human, not always perfect. Don't compare yourself to others. Value yourself.

Choices and thoughts forecast your life story.

Addictions temporarily ease inner pain, but they cause blurs, or wasted days, and cancel inner peace and self-worth.

Live with hope, faith, strength, love, and joy. No one can give you these qualities. It comes from within.

Since we cannot change reality,
Let us change the eyes which see reality.
Nikos Kazantzakis

Questions to Ponder

The stories we tell ourselves about who we are will become our truths.

What is the personal story you tell yourself?

How do others see you?

Who do you see in the mirror?

What does the word "self-respect" mean to you?

Remember three times when you felt good about yourself. Feel it and honor these experiences. It feed your soul.

What do you tolerate in your life? Does it nourish or distract from your joy?

Can you change the situation? Would a different mindset make a difference?

What words or actions from the past still influence your life today?

Do they promote or diminish your self-value? If negative, why do you hang on to them?

What are your personal strengths?

What three actions can you take to create more inner peace and fulfillment in your life?

Name three things you're grateful for in your life.

Did anything in Helen's spirit download resonate or impact the way you view your life?

It's your story. Only you can write the script.

Until you value yourself, you won't value your time
Until you value your time, you will not do anything
with it.
Scott Peck

The worst loneliness is to not be comfortable with
yourself.
Mark Twain

Chapter 12

Martin, the Spirit of a Famous Actor

"Take the Time to Truly Care, We Hide Our Pain Under a Mask."

Many of the messages from the world of spirit reveal a common thread that hinders life on Earth: lack of self-appreciation. Motivational speakers, countless books, articles, and other resources teach the importance of self-worth. Although people listen, families' and friends' opinions and judgments dominate their thoughts and actions. Individuality hides in a box, out of sight.

Bronnie Ware, author of *The Top Five Regrets of the Dying*, worked as a nurse and cared for patients during their final twelve weeks of life. According to Ware, the number one regret of people at the end of life is "I wish I'd had the courage to live a life true to myself, not the life others expected of me."

The spirit of a famous actor shared a message through me which echoed Ms. Ware's concept: Live life true to you, without later regrets. I changed the name of the actor to *Martin*. The spirit's transmitted words and validations were not altered and supported the facts I discovered through my research about the performer's life.

This actor entertained the world with his wit and humor. The roles he enacted on the screen highlighted the dignity all people deserve and crave. Martin's spirit emphasized this belief. I sense the actor's own life reflected a different story.

September 12, 2014, 5:52 AM

A restless and muffled chatter pushed me out of a peaceful sleep. With sleepy eyes, I glanced around the room for the disturbance. A soft glow in the corner of the room caught my attention in the semi-dark room. The volume of the mumbling increased, not from the room, but in my mind.

Moments of alertness triggered an instinctive knowing of an incoming spirit message. This initiated a spontaneous action to reach for a pen and notebook on the antique table next to my bed. As I scribbled the incoming words, I drifted into a semiconscious state. This resembles the way thoughts fade as sleep gently swallows the senses.

Martin's spirit's transmitted message:

The veil is thin, the whispers get louder
Voices are clamoring to come through
The rainbow speaks in colors to be heard
I am one with all—all one voice—no different
Don't single me out
Why not hear—don't doubt
Others talk, you write
Trust, believe
The I is really we—the we is just louder than the single voice
In our hearts the message is the same
Notice me for who I am
See me, look at me, speak to me—not the clown
The cries get louder
What can I do, you ask
Nurse me back to health
Understand my pain.
See my pain
Look at me

Look at my eyes
They reflect my soul
When my light is dim, notice, ask, see me
The clown can take over the ruse
That is what I've learned to do—early, in fact
The clown can disguise pain seen only to himself
Take the time to truly care, we hide it under the mask
Is it fair to play this game you ask?
We know no other way
Don't judge me
For no one is to blame
Just see me
Love me
Notice me
We are all one
Here on a discovery to oneness
The seas are blue
The ripples are strong
The tides slow down
The end of the wave is near
Do not cry
I made you laugh
The final act came down
My doing, the clown was through
Peace at last
It is true
See me now
The clown is gone
Me, really me, is near
Soon, soon, you will hear more
The scene now is clear
The whispers will get louder.

I originally named this spirit message the "Unidentified Clown Channel." After rereading the communication several times, the actor's name vibrated through my senses and negated logic. The phrase,

"Don't doubt, others talk, you write, trust, believe" made sense to me. Silently I questioned why this well-known actor's spirit came through to me. I wasn't a fan, didn't follow his career, and watched only one of his movies.

I asked Martin's spirit for three validations to indicate that he authored this download. If a departed soul prompted a willingness on my part to transcribe a message from another realm without questions, the spirit also knew how to arrange validations that clouded rational thought.

The first validation came nine days later. On September 21st, I walked past the living room, glanced at the TV, and saw Martin and a young boy walking down a dirt path. A closer look at the actor's eyes revealed the sadness described in the channeled message. A coincidence? Probably. The incident faded from my thoughts.

Within two days, on September 23rd, the following incident resembled a déjà vu experience. From the kitchen, I noticed another of Martin's movies on the television while my husband talked on the phone in another room. This time the screen presented an image of a younger Martin, along with his movie wife and children. It seemed odd. My husband and I rarely turn on the TV during the day. Another fluke?

At the end of a Pilates class the next morning, a meditation transported my consciousness to a trance state, similar to a light dream. The essence of many spirits floated in and out of my mind. Martin's image emerged. A clown mask covered his face. Amused, I mentally told his spirit, "You're going to have to do better than that." Moments later, I returned to full consciousness. The vision of Martin remained vivid and etched in my memory.

An hour later, I met a friend for coffee. She said, "Any visitations lately?" I'd barely uttered the words, "unidentified clown channel," when Alisa abruptly responded, "Did you see the chalk painting of a clown on exhibit in the downtown area?" Her phone landed in my hand. A photo with the likeness of Martin, disguised in a clown mask, smiled back at me.

I conceded. Three unusual incidents within four days, all with images of Martin, fell definitively into the validation category. I changed "The Unidentified Clown Channel" to "Martin's Message." I began my research to bring clarity to the channeled words.

Martin's laughter, light, and loving attitude through his movies generated worldwide admiration. But did people only see the actor, not the real person? I believe Martin's spirit informed us that his soul transitioned to a state of self-acceptance and peace. He no longer needs the mask.

Regardless of your beliefs about the reliability of Martin's downloaded message, the underlying tone of these channeled words shouts respect for self and others. It summarizes the meaning of authenticity, acceptance, and harmony with others. Many of the actor's diverse roles on stage and in film, his public appearances, and quotes while on Earth support and underscore the interdimensional spirit words.

Martin's Life Supported the Interdimensional Communication Received from Spirit

The channeled words, "The clown can take over the ruse. That is what I've learned to do—early," depicted how Martin first learned to act. In an interview with a well-known magazine, he shared how, at an early age, his mother acted silly when she played with him. Martin reacted with charm—another way to say, "Love me." He discovered how to make connections with people; he entertained.

Martin credited his father for the confidence to discuss controversial topics that affected society. The actor's compassion, humor, and sincerity brought depth to issues that embraced our hearts and emotions. His spirit message embodied this same trait. The richness of his channeled words continues to highlight the dignity and importance of each person. "Take the time to truly care."

My interpretation of the spirit words, "The rainbow speaks in colors to be heard," underlines a topic that evokes emotions in today's culture. Seven individual colors blend to create one rainbow. The spirit's message reminds us that *all* people, regardless of color, gender, sexual orientation, religion, political views, or social status, are equal. The transmitted words support an important message about tolerance and harmony. I feel Martin's declarations from the afterlife are essential today: "We are all one, here on a discovery to oneness. Don't single me out."

I feel the phrase in the download, "The seas are blue, the ripples are strong," describes the ups and downs in life. Even when life appears peaceful, an undercurrent of turmoil or distractions may erupt at any moment. How we respond produces a ripple effect throughout our lives and those around us. Discomfort, challenges, and daily existence change with time: "The tides slow down, the end of the wave is near."

The phrase, "The I is really we—the we is just louder than the single voice" repeats the theme of Martin's download and envelops everyone's secret desire, "Notice me for who I am."

From the youngest to the eldest, each of us desire and crave acceptance. Why do we feel the need to mimic others or to insist that people agree with our thoughts, beliefs, or way of life? The spirit message is clear: Take off your mask and let your uniqueness show. Allow others to do the same.

You may ask, "How can I help others?"

"Nurse them back to health."

"How?" You may ask.

"Notice them for who they are. Look at them. See them. Not the person they pretend to be."

Ways to Live an Authentic Life, According to Martin

- *Make decisions that align with your values, beliefs, morals, and needs.*

- *Listen to your inner voice, gut, and heart.*

- *Know your boundaries. Walk away from toxic people or situations.*

- *Communicate honesty with kindness and respect for others.*

- *Accept and like yourself. Have the courage to share your uniqueness with others.*

- *Take responsibility for your actions, both the good and the mistakes.*

- *Always being safe or hiding behind a mask hinders self-worthiness.*

- *To live a life true to yourself takes practice. It's a muscle that needs to be developed.*

Questions to Ponder

Authenticity is an expression of your true self, without masks. It's the freedom to be yourself.

How would you describe your true self without a mask?

Are you true to your core values and beliefs?

Describe your best qualities.

Which of these qualities are often not seen by others? Why?

What do you value most in life?

When are you the happiest and at peace?

When can you express your true self and feelings?

How do you hide your emotions? Why?

What three changes could you implement to become more authentic and sincere with yourself?

Did any words from Martin's spirit download resonate with you? How or why?

When was the last time you truly looked into a person's eyes? Did you notice their light, frustration, or dullness?

The privilege of a lifetime is to become who you truly are.
Carl Jung

Chapter 13
An Invasion of Red Ants

The first Sunday of daylight saving time toys with my emotions. Longer sun-filled days and less sleep create a lethargic feeling, much like a bear adjusting to its environment after winter's hibernation. Energy from a full moon magnifies my moods, sensitivities, and indecisiveness.

This Sunday was no exception. The anticipation of our weekly Developmental Mediumship Circle that evening created a restlessness. Self-doubts about the ability to make spirit contact are normal, but this day felt different. Thoughts wavered back and forth about whether I should attend the meeting. I decided to stay home.

An hour before the scheduled meeting, edginess increased. *Guilt*, I analyzed. Unable to sit still or focus, I grabbed my lipstick, purse, and sweater and rushed out the door.

I noticed more cars than usual in the parking lot and realized our group of eight had grown to fourteen participants when I entered the room. Nervous laughter, quick banters, and glances around the circle highlighted the silent question marks that saturated the air.

The facilitator opened the meeting with a brief description of the evening events and guidelines for the mediumship circle. Soft, angelic music played in the background and created an ambiance for the guided meditation. A sense of nausea caught me off guard. I second-guessed my hasty decision to join the group this evening. Gradually, my noisy thoughts went into silent mode.

An insect crawled across my arm five minutes into meditation. Without opening my eyes, I brushed it away. Within seconds, I sensed more trespassers. An invasion of red ants? I resisted the urge to leap out of my chair. Glanced down at my arm but saw nothing. An invisible sting of crisscross paths instigated a lightheadedness and my awareness of a spirit presence. *Not now*, I mentally commanded. Moments later, the annoyances stopped.

"The next activity involves working in pairs to deliver psychic impressions or spirit messages for your partner," the group leader announced.

I surveyed the room. A woman in her late twenties, dressed from the Gothic-punk era, caught my eye. Instinctively I knew my partner. Tension built while I watched the last few people paired.

"Our final team will be Tina and Maureen."

Tina's slumped posture differed from the air of defiance she attempted to project. The young woman straightened her lanky body and sauntered across the room. Thick, smoky eyeliner and deep velvet lips accentuated her sallow complexion. A weathered leather jacket, dark ripped mini skirt, and laced black tights conjured an image of a costume rather than regular attire. The sensitive brown eyes, hidden behind her dark makeup, were her ultimate betrayal.

Paths of burning sensations returned as Tina sank into the chair opposite me. I rubbed my arm over the invisible area of pain while I tried to make eye contact with my partner "Do you know someone who passed because of suicide?" The words seemed to fly out of my mouth without thought.

"No!"

The buzzing sound in my left ear shifted to a repetition of words that sounded like *cutter*.

Reluctantly, I asked, "Do you know anyone by the name of Carter?"

"No."

"I'm hearing the word Carter or cutter."

Tina's eyes widened. "My first boyfriend was a cutter. Allen didn't kill himself. It was an accident."

"What is a cutter?"

"Allen's childhood was terrible. He started cutting his arm at the age of fourteen. It made him feel better. When he couldn't shut off his memories or felt sad, he'd cut. It stopped his pain. I didn't understand it."

"How did he die?"

"I came home from work and found his crumpled and unconscious body on the living room floor. Allen died in the hospital. He never wanted to kill himself. He was only twenty-one. We were happy and wanted to be together." Tears streamed down her cheeks.

"It's strange," Tina said in a slow manner. "I remember a dream about Allen." Tina tilted her head to the side and stared into space.

"Two nights ago, I got really high with this guy. We had a fight, and I left. Must have passed out in my car. I remember Allen trying to wake me up in a dream. I think I nearly died. I was really messed up."

"Are you living with this man?"

"Not yet." Tina shifted her gaze to her hands. "I'm planning to move in with him next weekend."

A biblical image blinded my vision.

"Are you religious?" I asked.

She smirked. "Not anymore."

A biblical scene with Lot and his family, as they fled the city of Gomorrah, flashed in my mind. His wife looked frozen as she stared behind her. I also heard the words, 'Don't go back.'"

"Do you know this story from the Bible?" I asked.

"Not really."

"From what I remember, an angel told Lot to leave Gomorrah, a city of sin, with his family and warned them not to look back at its destruction. His wife ignored the advice and faced the city. She turned into a pillar of salt." I added, "You may want to search and read the story when you get home.

"I feel Allen's spirit showed me this powerful image to deliver the same message to you: Don't go back, move forward."

Tina folded her arms over her stomach and leaned forward. "I told my friend, the one I'm with this evening, about my plans. Liz felt it was a bad idea."

"Do you have another place to live?"

"Yes. Liz volunteered her place if I needed it." Tina continued, "She asked me to join her this evening since I've experienced some weird spirit stuff. I didn't want to come but finally agreed."

"The words *pinky fingers* continue to repeat in my mind. Those words mean anything to you?" I asked.

The young woman covered her face with her hands and quietly sobbed. Her body rocked back and forth. Through wet, dull eyes, she said, "That's what Allen and I always said to each other when we wanted the other person to keep a promise or to do something."

Tina held up her small finger, and we interlocked our pinky fingers.

Her voice cracked. "Pinky finger promise." Tears, stained with black eye makeup, flowed down her cheeks as she forced a smile. "I won't go back to his house."

To be or not to be, that is the question.
William Shakespeare

I'm not sure about Tina's background. Her heavy alcohol and drug use, insecurities, posture, clothes, defensive attitude, and eyes depicted a tale of sadness. For me, this story demonstrated the continuation of love and the determination of spirit to intervene and deliver a well-timed message from the afterlife. I never saw Tina after this event, but I believe she kept the pinky promise to Allen's spirit.

Tina introduced me to the term *cutter*. When I retold this story through my writing and studied information on the subject, I began to understand the depth and complexity of this behavior in today's younger population. The incidental facts Tina shared with me summarize what I discovered through my research.

Nonsuicidal Self-injury Data

- Nonsuicidal self-injury (NSSI) most often occurs in secret to alleviate intense negative emotions. It involves deliberate and intentional injury to body tissue. Some examples include self-cutting and self-hitting.

- Even though when individuals engage in NSSI there is no deliberate intent to die or kill themselves, it is reported that 63% of students and 36% of adults who have engaged in NSSI have entertained suicidal thoughts.

- One-third of adolescents in the U.S. have engaged in non-suicidal self-harm. This consists of actions that cause pain to one's own body: pinching, scratching, hitting, banging, scraping, carving, or burning.

- Research shows 20 percent of college students have engaged in NSSI.

- Reports indicate it is a form of self-directed anger or self-punishment. It's more common in people prone to self-criticism.

- The action of self-injury brings feelings of relief and calm. It temporarily stops negative or emotionally charged feelings.

- The typical age to begin self-harm is thirteen to fourteen.

- Twenty-five percent of people who engage in NSSI also report eating disorders (anorexia or bulimia).

- The number of individuals who engage in nonsuicidal self-harm behavior is increasing. (This data is easily researched and while some numbers may vary, all information points to the reasons NSSI should not be ignored.)

The similarities between Tina's substance abuse and her spirit friend's behavioral patterns on Earth indicate a lack of self-control and feelings of unworthiness. When people have confidence, self-destructive behaviors are rarely tested. In this story, both Tina and her friend Allen found it easier to hide from their emotions than deal with them. Harmful cravings and habits develop into a blueprint for dependency and lead to shame and deterioration of pride.

Common Threads in the Earthly Existence of Martin (actor), Lenny (teenager, death by suicide), and Allen (cutter, self-injury)

- Disguises emotional pain.
- Hides behind a mask to cover individuality.
- Felt unappreciated, unseen, and not understood.
- Difficulty expressing their true self.
- Feelings of loneliness.
- Hurtful childhood or teenage memories.
- Low self-appreciation and worthiness.

Spirit Messages on Suicide and Self-harm Prevention

Martin's and Lenny's afterlife downloads provide essential advice for parents:

- *LISTEN and BE PRESENT. This is the best gift you can give to anyone, especially your child.*

- *"Notice me for who I am."*

- *"When the light is dim, notice, ask."*

- *"Nurse me back to health."*

- *"Don't judge me."*

- *"Just see me. Love me. Notice me."*

- *"Can disguise my pain seen only to myself."*

- *"We hide it (pain and individuality) under a mask."*

- *"Teach (the young) the value of their lives."*

- *"Teach (the young) they are perfect, don't need to please (others)."*

- *Model love, honesty, authenticity, respect, and acceptance of others. Walk your talk.*

- *Discuss solutions and coping skills.*

- *Seek professional help and guidance, if needed.*

Martin, Lenny, Tina, and Allen feared rejection if they lived authentically. The opinions of others influenced and dictated the story of their lives.

To be yourself in a world that is constantly trying to make you something else is the greatest accomplishment.
Ralph Waldo Emerson

Chapter 14
Self-bullying: Hit the Delete Button

Today, people are aware of bullying within schools, work environments, places of worship, and families. Educational curricula, human resource regulations, and outreach programs offer guidance and education to reduce the victimhood and mental anguish of its intended targets.

An area that receives less attention is *self*-bullying or negative self-talk. It involves the same emotional pain and fear and paralyzes motivation and life choices. We know bullies intimidate and try to weaken a person's defense and self-perception. Yet we silently allow our inner dialogue to criticize or put down and devalue our self-worth. This takes many forms; often, it reflects insecurities, fears, and cynical core beliefs. It resides in assumptions, not facts or truth. Some common examples may include some of the following:

I always…

I'm…

I can't…

I'm not enough

It's my fault that…

Or when directed at self, it may sound something like the following:

Stop being a baby.

Get over it.

You are being so…

What an idiot, you should have known...

Of course you would mess this up too...

That was stupid for you to think...

And on and on. Consider this: Would you speak to a friend or a child in need like this? Why would you speak to yourself this way?

When and where did we inhale thoughts of imperfection or a less-than attitude? Babies and young children are adventurous, fearless, and joyful as they explore and interact with their surroundings. This slowly changes as remarks and conditioning from family, educators, religion, romantic partners, peers, and cultural and societal norms influence thoughts and self-perception. When we allow others to shape our identity, our uniqueness fades.

Lessons and the positive side of life's challenges often take the back seat, while unpleasant memories lead the way and steer our self-image. If we hit the delete button every time a self-limiting word pops into our mind and replace it with a reaffirming or what-if statement, we change our thoughts' energy, pattern, and influence.

Some examples:

I am persistent and disciplined in breaking the habit of...

I am worthy of respect and acceptance.

I attract healthy and positive people in my life.

Every day I am becoming healthier and stronger in...

I am capable of...

I learned from... and choose to...

What-if statements ignite a mindset that embraces change and possibilities rather than limitations.

What if I let go of fear to... just for today?

What if I am worthy of love and happiness, I'd...?

What if I took one step toward... every day or this week?

What if I commit to...?

What if I stop assuming the outcome and try to...?

What if I challenge myself to...?

Stand up and protect yourself from the bully within. Don't let it destroy your confidence and block peace and happiness. Take control of your life. Change the landscape and outcome of tomorrow: delete, delete, *delete*.

The four celebrities in this book entertained the world with their creativity, intelligence, talent, passion, and dynamic presence. In their private life, insecurities and challenges mimicked those of the general population. Money and fame couldn't buy self-worth or silence their inner critic, so we can only imagine how hard it is for the average person.

Interdimensional Reflections and Guidance from the Afterlife:

Helen: Voices (within my head) pierce my silence, can't stop. Stillness (or peace) never comes without a price.

The singer's guidance from beyond: Find a new song from the heart. Change the course (the words you tell yourself).

* * *

Daniel: There are no more rational thoughts, just the decay of the mind. He (the joker of life) lives in the mind that succumbs to the false hope of peace, helplessness, and faded dreams.

The actor's spirit guidance from beyond: If only for a moment light came and maybe, just maybe, a glimmer of hope (for change). Go beyond limiting thoughts and perceptions.

* * *

Tommy: Visions of yesterday fade, drink some more. The bottle of hidden peace and surrenders to vanity and lost tomorrows.

The musician's spirit words of guidance: The disease of pain destroys. Let go of the past hurts, it destroys the soul.

* * *

Martin: The clown can take over the ruse. That is what I've learned to do early, in fact.

The actor's spirit guidance from beyond: Take off your mask. Show yourself.

* * *

Don't allow your bullying voice to win! Negative self-talk distorts your reality. Awareness of discouraging thought patterns is the first step toward empowerment. Delete hurtful comments and replace them with an optimistic statement. The time to make changes is now.

Questions to Ponder

What situations or people trigger self-doubt or negative self-criticism?

Are these thoughts based on facts, feelings, or assumptions?

What would you tell a relative or friend if they engaged in the same self-talk that you say to yourself?

Is there a pattern or situation that triggers negative self-talk?

How do these thoughts affect your behavior or moods?

What can you do to change this pattern and not engage in self-negativity?

How often do you use the word *can't*?

List three things in your life that motivate you to change.

Prioritize your three motivators.

Describe yourself using five positive words. How do you share these qualities with others?

List three or more things you are grateful for at this moment.

Did any words resonate with you from this section?

Chapter 15
Rewards of Forgiveness

Many spirit messages reveal the unwillingness to forgive others. It affected their spiritual, mental, and physical bodies while on Earth. People encounter this same dilemma today: to forgive or not to forgive. Unfortunately, pride manufactures a victory badge and creates a false sense of power over the offender, living or deceased. Untying this status symbol from feelings of righteousness often creates a loss of entitlement.

In the next interdimensional communication, The Collective Voice summarizes the rewards of forgiveness. Initially, I decided not to use the download in this book. When I finished writing the chapter, a mental nudge drew my attention back to the passage.

The Rewards of Forgiveness, viewed from the spirit realm, may be worth consideration.

The Rewards of Forgiveness

Channeled April 2, 2015

Many thoughts, many minds, many messages
We all come together to join the legion of the masses
The freedom is divine
The peacefulness is bliss
When the time is right
The morning dew will lift you up to reunite

The milk of the breast feeds many
The kingdom of heaven spreads a table of the wealth
A wealth some are denied
Learning, weeping from pain
Gather your wit
See the wealth of the land and messages in all forms
Learn now, keep the faith
We are all one joined in love and peace
Forgive now, don't wait, the cries of all are heard
Harden not your heart
The peace marches into the heart
Lifts the kindred spirit and jumps in joy
Why wait—the rewards are many
Peace and love flow through
Forgive
The time has come to open and join a few
Many lands, many adventures of the soul yet to come
Release now the lessons, the burden of the heart
We are near, gather your wit, make the plunge
Fill your heart with love, hold not to hatred, let it go
Serve the spirit of the soul
Much to learn, much to gain
Release, my love, the pain
Yesterday is gone
The new day brings the sun
Let it shine in the dawn
Let the joy come through
Many souls reveal the path
Open your hearts, hear with your hearts
The music of the Lord
Dance to the rhythm of the soul
Listen, the time is near, much will be revealed
Lighten the spirit
Join the light
Let the power of God lead the way

Surrender to the ways of the land
Forgive, love, and pray
Play comes when the fruit of our labor rejoices in the heart
Release the pain that freezes the mind
Laugh the joy of hope
Simple truths
The task is for all

Author—A Collective of Souls

How few there are who have courage enough to own their faults, or resolution enough to mend them.
Benjamin Franklin

Chapter 16
The Ping-pong Challenge

It didn't take long to learn about spirits' determination and obstinance when they want to make contact with a loved one on Earth.

"Hi Sam, I've decided to sell my house. Since you're the best real estate agent in town, I'd like to talk about listing it with your company."

"Sure. Are you available this Sunday around 1:00 p.m.? Be good to see you again. Been five years?"

"Six years since you and Ryan joined us for Thanksgiving. Sam, sorry to hear about your son's death. How are you doing?"

"It's been a long, difficult two years since Ryan's sudden passing. He was only thirty-four. Wish I'd done things differently."

Memories of Thanksgiving surfaced soon after our conversation. Ryan's gregarious smile and playful competitiveness monopolized the lead in most of our ping-pong challenges before and after dinner. His reliance on prescription medications for chronic back pain didn't hinder him.

Over the next two days, images and thoughts of Ryan played like a broken record. Didn't think anything unusual since this was my only encounter with the young man and the last time I saw Sam.

An hour before Sam's arrival, a familiar agitation increased. I tried to blink away a vivid picture of Ryan in my mind's eye. Tingles crawled up and down the side of my face. Spirit was close. Insecurities began to mount. Too much knowledge about the family could sabotage the purity of a spirit message if I unconsciously injected my own thoughts. I jogged around the backyard with the hope to provide a physical and mental distraction.

After two laps, a high-pitched vibrational sound pierced my ear. Ready or not, a spirit communication flowed through my mind. I grabbed the notepad from the patio table and scribbled down the incoming words.

Doubts turned loud when the utterances ceased. Few people knew my secret life. Sam wasn't one of them. He would view any form of paranormal activity with a chuckle and dismiss the evidence as impossible or made up. I understood. My logic runs the same way until the spirit words are validated and provide value for the receiver.

Without warning, my back and right knee felt a discomfort so severe I grabbed the table and dropped inches from the ground. *What happened?* Scoliosis and arthritis reared their nasty heads from time to time, but this felt like someone swung at me with a heavy rod. When I realized the pain wasn't mine and acknowledged it belonged to Ryan while on Earth, it stopped. Sam drove up the driveway at that exact moment.

After warm greetings, we shared highlights from the last several years with a blend of humor and sarcasm. The conversation faded when we approached the glass French doors that led to the patio and yard. The silence spoke volumes.

Sam exhaled a slow, heavy sigh, "I can still picture Ryan and our ping-pong challenges on Thanksgiving. It seems so long ago."

The air turned cold despite the 100-degree temperature. I bit my bottom lip to calm the racing images. Heart palpitations triggered an adrenaline rush. All fears about revealing the recent spirit encounter disappeared. The disclosure of Ryan's recent visitation gushed out of my mouth. Sam turned, stared at me in bewilderment, and plopped onto a nearby chair while I read the words his son's spirit delivered.

My friend slowly glanced around the room as if to search for a rational explanation. In a tone that conveyed mental exhaustion, Sam confirmed most of the evidence relayed by Ryan's spirit. The pain I experienced in my back and right knee replicated his son's description while he was alive.

Sam's grief had eased over the past two years, but the night of his son's passing still haunted him. On that evening, the young man complained of chest pain. Familiar with the habitual health moans from his son, Sam tried to pacify him and said they'd seek medical assistance in the morning if the pain persisted. Flu-like symptoms for the past three days drained Sam's energy; he craved sleep.

Ryan passed from heart failure during the night, or as Ryan's spirit channeled, "a swollen heart."

My friend blamed himself for his son's death. The stress showed throughout his body. I believe the spirit's relentless pursuit to be heard rests within these words: *"Tell him there was nothing he could have done. I love him."*

Every interdimensional communication I receive from a spirit reflects pure love, without attached strings or conditions. Ryan's spirit visitation reminds us that our loved ones in spirit are around, especially in times of pain and struggle. These souls send words to free us of guilt, heal our hearts, and remind us to live in the present moment. The heart connection continues beyond physical existence.

Where there is great love,
there are always miracles.
Willa Cather

Questions to Ponder

Have you lost a friend or loved one suddenly or unexpectedly?

What thoughts about this person cause the most pain or sorrow?

What were your happiest memories with this person?

How has this death affected you emotionally, physically, or spiritually?

What would you say to this person today?

Sometimes journaling about your feelings or writing a letter to the person will help with the grief.

How could someone support you with your sorrow?

What would the departed person tell you or wish for you in this present moment?

Chapter 17

A Spirit's Chilly Message

The unconscious weight of past wounds triggers emotional irritations, while the real source lies comatose, covered with excuses and blame. Many times, the inability to forgive another or ourselves causes this mindset. Until we acknowledge a problem exists, change seldom follows.

A Spirit's Chilling Intervention

I met Catherine for the first time when she walked into my office for a Human Design reading. Based on the time, day, and location of birth, this type of chart reveals inherited traits from ancestors, personality characteristics, and an individual's strengths and challenges. Catherine found the information useful. A few months later she called to set up a Human Design appointment for her husband, Dylan.

The morning of Dylan's appointment, an eerie picture of a wooden handle ice pick appeared in my dream. The realism of the image jolted me from sleep. An uneasiness accompanied questions. *Why did the image appear vivid and real? Was it a dream?* A pale light in the corner of my room caught my attention as I heard the words telepathically: "Tell Dylan about the ice pick. It's important."

Sensing the energy in the room, I instinctively recognized the spirit of Dylan's mother. I responded through my thoughts. *You provide the opportunity, and I'll bring the ice pick image into the conversation.*

Dylan's mother, Joey, had passed two years earlier. Her spirit delivered messages through me during a mediumship reading with Catherine. This soul imparted a distinctive mother energy. Her witty and colorful presence mirrored her life on Earth. According to her daughter-in-law Dylan and their oldest daughter inherited the mother's intuitive instincts. Many times, they felt her comforting presence. Information in Dylan's Human Design chart supported these supernatural abilities.

Catherine, Dylan, and their two children arrived at my office the afternoon of the spirit's early morning visitation. Ten minutes into the discussion of Dylan's chart, it seemed apparent to me that Catherine had dragged her husband to this appointment. His team shirt and excitement for the football playoffs that afternoon turned his chart information into humdrum chatter.

I felt our meeting needed to end or be rescheduled. When I opened my mouth to voice my concern, an element in Dylan's chart design caught my attention: Gate 48, the gate of depth. People with this trait are more inclined to hold on to fears and hide feelings of inadequacy. Many times, parental conditioning lies at the root of these mindsets. A strong urge to discuss this one area overpowered my plan to continue the meeting later.

After a brief explanation of the trait, I asked Dylan if he connected to the information. A cold chill materialized in the room. The sudden appearance of the ice pick image reappeared in my mind's eye and fogged my thoughts.

"Does an ice pick mean anything to you?" I blurted out.

Dylan and Catherine stared at each other. Dylan stiffened; his face turned a shade lighter. He responded in a low tone.

"The ice pick could mean two, maybe three, things to me."

"Your mother's spirit showed me an image of an ice pick with a wooden handle this morning."

"My father's mental and verbal abuse created friction in the family." Dylan continued, "Before Mother's death, she told me to chip away at the ice that formed around my heart."

"I feel your mother's spirit came through me to remind you of her words."

Catherine quietly told her husband, "You need to hear this." She took her daughters' hands and led them outside.

"It's hard to forget the way my father treated me. His words always felt hurtful and harsh." After moments of silence he added, "Sometimes, I act the same way. I don't want that for my family."

Slumped on the couch, Dylan stared at his hands as if they somehow held the answer for transformation. Reflection on his own actions exposed the wisdom behind the words spoken by his mother years earlier.

Gradually, he recognized how his inner agitation and turmoil triggered unconscious responses to situations or challenges. It takes courage, humility, and determination to peer deep into the depths of the heart and acknowledge a sincere desire to change.

I felt Dylan's mother's larger-than-life personality on the physical plane, and now in spirit, arranged the unraveling of insights, coincidences, and events during this and my previous meetings with her daughter-in-law. Loved ones in the afterlife want us to live life fully and without regrets. This motherly soul intervened when her son and his family could understand how the influences of unconscious conditioning from other people cause undercurrents in life. Delving deep into the well of hidden emotions and hurt initiates a path toward mental, spiritual, and physical healing.

This is certain, that a man that studieth revenge
keeps
his wounds green, which otherwise would heal and
do well.
Francis Bacon

Chapter 18
Choices Have Consequences

Suicide may be a personal choice, but it affects family, friends, coworkers, and acquaintances. The following story reveals how anguish and emotional ache ruin the lives and the well-being of survivors.

For the past several years, I've attended Mediumship Development Circles. People with various levels of psychic and mediumship skills come together on a regular basis. The members rarely share personal information. This makes it easier for the medium to relay a message from the spirit world without the filter of preconceived knowledge about another person.

Ten minutes before the start of the Development Circle, Peter, a regular member of the group, entered the room and stormed toward me. He handed me a photograph and roared, "Tell me about him." His attitude stunned everyone in the room.

Before I had a chance to respond or look at the photograph, a white banner projected the word *forgiveness* in my mind.

Cautiously I replied, "There's an empty seat beside me, Peter. We can discuss this after meditation or, if you'd prefer, in private."

The group leader's guided meditation and music turned down the noise of negativity in the room, and serenity returned.

In meditation, I saw the word *forgiveness* intensify to exaggerated proportions across my third eye's vision. When meditation ended, I looked at Peter's photo. Sadness enveloped me. This was a picture of Peter's father. The visions and spirit messages I heard unraveled the circumstances that led to this man's passing.

After meditation, members of the group share the insights or spirit visitations they received.

In a quiet tone, I asked Peter, "I believe the spirit of your father came through to me. Do you want to hear his message now or later after the meeting?"

"Now," he rasped in response.

Peter leaned forward in his chair. His eyes, dark with anger, glared at me. A slight show of emotion crept through his icy stare when Peter heard his father's spirit talk about the mediumship skills of Peter's young daughter.

"I want him to stay away from my family," Peter's voice vibrated with rage.

These words confirmed the words Peter had heard from his five-year-old daughter that morning: "Grandpa plays with me."

The reason the forgiveness banner appeared massive in my mind made sense. The father's suicide had shocked his family. They dealt with grief and loss daily. The anguish in Peter's heart remained raw with anger and hurt.

Neither Peter nor I mentioned the word *suicide* in any verbal exchange, but our eyes revealed the truth, visible only to us.

The father's spirit conveyed the despair and hopelessness he experienced before his death. Life lost meaning. Pride and shame kept Peter's father from sharing his feelings with anyone, especially his family.

Hopefully, sometime in the future, Peter will reconsider his father's appeals for forgiveness. This will allow Peter to begin the healing process and heal the ache that gnaws at his life.

Questions to Ponder

Do you know a person who struggled with challenges, numbness, loneliness, and defeat and has transitioned?

What are your favorite memories of this person?

What do you wish they had known?

What three descriptive words describe your pain or sorrow?

Have you had thoughts that life is too difficult and not worth the struggles it brings?

What triggers these thoughts?

Who would be the most affected by your early death?

How would your death impact the emotional, physical, and spiritual life of people left behind?

Do you feel the person who chose early death by suicide, alcohol, drugs, or self-harm realized it's a final departure from this life and the effect it had on the survivors?

Did anything in Peter's story, Choices Have Consequences, stand out or resonate with you? Why?

Chapter 19
My March Down the Dark Corridor to Forgiveness—Part II

Forgiveness is a decision to let go of blame, resentment, or anger from a perceived offense or hurt. The conscious effort to forgive aligns with most religious and spiritual practices throughout the world. It took three additional years, after my mandated DUI classes, to march down the corridor toward forgiveness. My heart opened and allowed images of yesteryear to fade many times, but it closed again if someone mentioned my mother's name.

The disease of pain gradually lifted. My emotional eyesight improved, loved ones became more visible. The ripple effects of forgiveness launched stages of enlightenment and personal growth that continue to evolve today. Spirit downloads, channeling, mediumship, and a closer relationship and trust in God came to the forefront of my life. It guided the development of this manuscript.

A year after I changed the words in my story and allowed blame, anger, and hurt from my childhood to dissolve, a medium in our development circle relayed a message from the other side.

"The spirit of your mother is here. She wants to thank you for forgiving her and shows me a gold heart in her outstretched hands." I placed my hands over my chest and closed my eyes to embed the vision in my heart.

Three months after that incident, a friend handed me an elegant gift bag on my birthday. "I felt this would be the perfect gift for you."

Nestled inside iridescent tissue paper, I discovered a replica of the gold heart my mind had visualized months earlier. The bag also included a coffee mug inscribed with the words "A Heart of Gold" sketched within a large golden heart.

Neither the medium nor my friend knew about Mother. Soon after, hearts appeared at random times and places. They turned into Mother's spirit's personal calling card and a reminder of her love from the invisible world.

Forgiveness changed the trajectory of my life. Inner freedom and peace allowed light to flow in and seal the wounds from the past. I can't change my childhood, but I can redesign the story I tell myself. Forgiveness materialized into a gift of tenderness for me and revealed a fresher and freer view of life.

A passage from the Lord's Prayer contains these words: "Forgive us our trespasses as we forgive those who trespass against us." Although I recited the prayer regularly and felt the words in my heart, my actions and thoughts conveyed a different message: The pain of my childhood hurts, I won't release it.

God grant me the serenity to accept the things I
cannot change, the courage to change the things I
can, and the wisdom to know the difference.
Reinhold Niebuhr

Questions to Ponder

How would you define forgiveness?

What do the words "I'm sorry" mean when you say or hear them from another person?

Have you witnessed the effects of someone who could not or would not forgive?

How did it affect their life or relationships?

Have you experienced too much hurt or anger to forgive? How much does it control your thoughts, conversations, or actions?

What made it personal? (This means personal to you only, through your own thoughts and perceptions.)

Did it elicit emotions or memories from your childhood?

Are you carrying or reacting to the "baggage" of another? (The anger, frustrations, emotional stuff that's not yours.)

What words or actions from the past still influence your life today?

Do they promote or diminish your self-value? If negative, why do you hang on to them?

What three actions can you take to create more inner peace and fulfillment in your life?

Soul's Growth Exercise

Imagine you have one week to live.

What one thing would you change in your life?

Would there be unfinished business regarding forgiveness in your life?

What would you ask God or Creator to forgive in your life?

The strongest principle of growth lies in human choice.
George Eliot

Chapter 20
Arthur Findlay College

October 2013

I will never forgive my mother and will take this promise to the grave," snapped a timid woman in her early sixties. "Knowing Mother, she's probably gloating in the afterlife that her daughter is a medium," Anna continued.

The outburst caught me and others by surprise. Anna sat at our meal table for the past five days, rarely spoke, and occasionally shared a vacant smile.

The surge of emotion occurred during breakfast on the sixth and final day of mediumship development at the renowned College of Spirit and Psychic Studies. Joyful voices filled the room while student-mediums reveled in their success with spirit communications. This loud outburst of fury stunned our table of eight. Talking stopped. All eyes focused on Anna as she continued her rant.

"Mother tried to contact me through three different mediums. I refused to hear anything from that woman and insisted her spirit be sent away," Anna snapped.

The woman's pallid complexion, slumped posture, and pursed lips revealed bitterness and pain. No one knew how to respond. She had maintained an invisible presence at our table for five days.

The mass exit around us didn't faze Anna. She sat motionless and continued to gaze into space. After people scurried out the door to morning meditation, I said, "Anna, would you like to talk about it now or later?"

Anna growled, "I grew up in a strict religious environment, home-schooled, and not allowed friends. Mother's verbal abuse and harsh rules dominated my life. Turned worse after Dad passed."

"Do you have brothers or sisters?"

"No! Mother didn't want children, and she didn't want me! Mother was a bitter and angry person. She never shared anything about her childhood or life. It seemed beneath her to discuss feelings or show love."

Pain from the past oozed through every cell of this woman's fragile frame. Sadness and unworthiness surged through her words.

"She's probably sitting next to me, smirking that she's at Arthur Findlay College with her daughter."

Chills raced through my body. An energy form of an older woman materialized in my mind. The spirit of Anna's mother validated her daughter's words.

"It's been fifteen years since her death; nothing from her until now."

Anna had attended many courses at Arthur Findlay over the years while she pursued a psychic mediumship career. She had to realize that, at some point, her mother could channel through another medium. Did fear of more rejection initiate Anna's outburst? Aside from a few ladies cleaning the tables, Anna and I were the only students in the dining hall.

I listened while this person unleashed a lifetime of declarations that surrounded emotional abandonment and feelings of unworthiness.

"Have you thought about speaking to a professional or minister?"

"No! It's expensive and I'm not religious!" Tears filled her eyes. "I'm not good at talking about my life with others."

"Anna, you've been through a lot, and I don't know everything you've experienced, but I see your pain. If you don't mind, I'd like to share what I've learned about forgiveness and feelings of abandonment."

With a sigh, lips pressed together, and a quivering chin, she nodded while staring at her hands.

I recalled the humiliating experience of my DUI and questions I had about why my mother preferred the numbness of alcohol over her relationship with family and life. I also told her about Mother's spirit visitation through a medium.

During the difficult process of changing my attitude from victimhood to forgiving, I experienced a dream visitation from my mother. At 4:00 a.m., I woke up to the words, "Peace is forgiveness. Forgiveness is peace." The presence of my mother seemed real and close, but I couldn't see her.

Mentally I heard her say, "I'm sorry for the hurt I caused. I didn't want you. My selfishness blamed you for the life I couldn't have. Didn't appreciate my life. I suffered and lost. Proud of you, proud of all of you. I'm so sorry. I've learned a lot."

"Anna, when I removed the heavy cloak of numbness and anger it became easier to forgive Mother. At that point, my life changed. I started to like myself, see and value family and the people around me. Blame faded. It was a humbling experience."

"Thank you," the woman whispered as we went our separate ways to join morning classes.

Telepathically, I asked Mother's spirit for assistance from the other side. I didn't understand how souls related to one another in the afterlife, but maybe her spirit could intervene and help Anna's mother initiate the healing process between mother and daughter.

When I walked toward our lunch group three hours later, Anna appeared visibly different. Her smile wide, eyes glowing and fixed on mine, she burst into cheerful chatter.

"Two different mediums brought Mother's spirit through this morning. Both times she apologized for her bitterness and its impact on my life. She said she loved me!"

Words from her mother's spirit erased the hardness behind Anna's colorless complexion. Childlike glee radiated from her frail frame. This lady had nursed feelings of abandonment and unworthiness for fifty years. The arms of victimhood kept anger, blame, and resentment close to the heart and blocked the vitality of life. An earlier refusal to allow her mother's spirit to communicate indicated an entrenched fear of rejection. The practice of self-protection sharpens the art of self-denial.

Anna's message from the other side cranked open an old wooden door that unlocked the secret passage to heal. Her heart opened. This middle-aged woman received the approval and love that she craved from her mother.

The synchronicity and timing of Anna's outburst and struggle with hurt and rejection reaffirmed the golden heart of love my mother's spirit and I share. To this day, I feel Mother's invisible presence. I'm convinced she supports me from beyond to deliver messages of compassion, understanding, and forgiveness essential for family reconciliation and healing.

If we could read the secret history of our enemies,
we would find in each person's life sorrow and
suffering enough to disarm all hostility.
Henry Wadsworth Longfellow

Chapter 21

Train to Nowhere

Authored by Spirit

May 8, 2015, 3:29 AM

Train to Nowhere

Where is the train to Nowhere taking us?
Our bags are packed as we travel nowhere in our mind
The purpose is to get to the destination,
But where is Nowhere?
I see the movie with scenes of anger, unforgiveness set in the
background of darkness
The tunnel of blackness stills the mind—
Nowhere is the force that drives the way
Brief scenes are played with love and joy,
But why are these words uncomfortable to the soul?
The baggage is heavy, the daylight never comes
The nights are long on our way to Nowhere
Shed the bags, leave them behind you say?
But how will I survive on my trip to Nowhere?
Strip them from your hands, leave one behind,
Drop it for a while, lighten your load, take out the contents in the bag

Maybe you have outgrown the old clothes,
The old way of wearing the costume of choice?
Try the suit of anger on
Does it feel tight, bulky, or is it dirty with old stains?
Leave it behind, one less garment on your trip to Nowhere
The bag of unforgiveness is heavy, the straps are old, falling apart and
tearing
Open the bag. Find something long past the date of stylish wear
It's old, ugly, and hangs lifeless on the body
Leave it behind
Leave all the memories hanging on threads,
Remove them from the grip of buttons
Lighten your load my friend, the road to Nowhere is long
Check the lightness of the load that tires us on the road
Is that the sun starting to rise as the baggage is left behind?
The lightness of the load is freshness,
Where will it lead?
See the birds, hear the sounds,
Do we know the path out of Nowhere?
Lighten the load, one at a time, brings smiles and freshness that the
bags wore down
The trip to Nowhere has a new name, the name of a song I start to sing
Maybe, just maybe, the song of joy is free to show the way
Look my friend, a new train is near
Minimum baggage is required
The fee: Leave behind bags that bind and load the spine
The new train is called The Road to Freedom
The freedom to be me.

Authored by Spirit

Conclusion

My Dear Reader,

I appreciate that you allowed me to share ordinary, everyday narratives about the challenges in my life and guidance from the spirit world.

Many of us straddle paths that echo the ones laid out in these stories as we walk through corridors of shadows, complexities, self-doubt, and joys.

A common thread that infiltrated the spirit stories about authenticity, forgiveness, disease of pain, addictions, and suicide is self-sabotage/self-bullying. The words we tell ourselves matter. They weave the garment of beliefs that defines our essence and becomes our costume of choice.

My prayer and hope for this book is that some words or your personal reflections provide insight and motivation to reevaluate what is important in your life and worth the fight. You, alone, are the creator of your Earthly narrative. What story or footprint will you leave on the sands of time?

Simple wisdom from the afterlife:
Be you. Be empowered. Act. Discover you.
Live fully, without later regrets.

The following quote encapsulates timeless wisdom shared by spiritual, motivational platforms.

Look back and see experience.
Look forward and see hope.
Look around and see your reality.
Look within and find yourself.
Look up and find God.
Author Unknown

The Night Watchmen
"The Time to Heal Is Now"

The **Night Watchmen** spirit communication echoes the voices and sentiments of souls who died by suicide, an accident, or illness robbing them of a chance to say goodbye. These departed souls speak in one voice but with various tones. A heartfelt force behind the phrases reflects unearthly sentiments that beg for understanding, forgiveness, and a plea to heal now. The definition of a night watchman, according to the dictionary, is a person who serves as a guard at night and protects and warns of danger.

The Night Watchmen, October 16, 2014, 3:38 AM

A restless night produced thoughts fixated on the inability to fall asleep instead of the calmness that nurtures sleep. After long hours of tossing and turning, a faint chatter within my mind pried me from my restlessness. A conditioned reflex caused me to fumble for my pen and journal on the table beside my bed. The words flowed from my mind to the page without effort or full consciousness.

The Night Watchmen (First download)

The veil is thin tonight, much needs to come through
Hearts are restless, time is elusive, words are many
Please hear

The cries are getting louder
Much needs to be heard

To the survivor:

Shh my love, never meant to hurt, cry not for me
The whispers are heard
Time has come to heal the hurt, the mysteries are revealed

The heart opens, cries flow, the darkness is dispelled
See the light come in as sorrows vanish
Please bring in the peace

We are you
We are the Night Watchmen

To heal the soul takes courage and love
Face the demons, stand firm, they are as strong as your imagination or
belief
See the pain, feel the pain
Now let go and trust

Learn to love
Hear the words of sorrow
We are sorry for the pain, cannot undo
Please, listen is our plea

When the wind howls in the heart
The mind shuts down
The shadows dance with joy, "We have won"

Take back your strength
Pray from the heart
Melt the sorrow
Bring in the light
See the vapors of illusion disappear

The silence pierces the veil
We are all one
To each heart we come to join

See the birds, feel the wind
The water calms as one
I'm sorry, I'm so sorry yells from all
Let me help wipe the tears that flow from your heart

We wait to be heard
Don't turn your back
The swallows all come back
Little has been said about the whispers of the heart
Feel, believe, and trust

Open yourself up to the unseen world
Much will be revealed
It will make sense
Takes time for the mind to see the wisdom of the vine

Within the shadows of reality, the mist is lifting
Be aware
True value comes when you are awake and can see with the eyes of
wisdom and belief
The seed has been planted
Soon the harvest comes.

After I scribed the last word and while in a semiconscious state, I wandered into my office. More words started to pierce my mind with urgency for acknowledgment. As if sedated by the influx of incoming information, I flopped on a nearby chair. The words dodged cognitive recognition and unquestioningly flowed from the pen onto the pages of my journal.

October 16, 2014, 3:58 AM (Second download)

Messages to me:

Much is revealed when you pray and meditate—why do you wait?
Lead with your heart, much needs to be heard

The whispers grow louder when the pain never stops
We need to heal and cover the hearts with the tapestry of love

Woven in layers of forgiveness, hope, and a desire to be whole once more
Those that need healing will take refuge a little at a time until the heart gently heals
Our army of soldiers march to the field to be heard by many

Please tell them we are near, we love them
And will try to protect their heart from bleeding more
Tell them to trust, let go of guilt and entitlement to their pain – it never heals at this point

Messages to the survivors:

The light we carry heals
As we gradually heal from the Earthly realm
We see the physical pain left behind
"So sorry" can be meaninglessly understood
But please my loved ones, open your hearts
The time to heal is now

Much will be revealed as time marches on and the heavens open to receive you
Until that time, please know I am with you, guiding, massaging your thoughts and heart
We have little voice
Our love comes through the pen in physical reality

Listen
Open your choice to receive or reject
Please, my love, listen and judge not
I am sorry, I am sorry, I am sorry
Do not delete

It is only when you release sorrow in your heart that both of us are set free
I love you, remember that
Set us both free
The physical world is brilliant

Not always seen from your Earthly perspective
From where I am, it shines like the many stars of heaven
Please revere the beauty of your palace

My friends and loved ones
Stop, reflect, and pray anyway that you respect
We are all one

My love continues from a place not known to you now
Believe I am near
Please release the pain and doubt

I am near

My love grows to a depth that the physical world does not understand
My mission is done on the physical plane
Yours is yet to become reality

Live, love, and trust

These messages insinuate souls on the other side see and feel the pain of loved ones left behind. The download carries various interpretations, deciphered by the needs of each intended beneficiary of the spirit words.

This channel spoke to me about my insecurities and hesitancy to deliver messages I received from the other side. My grandmother's harsh warning, "Keep spirit things to yourself. People will call it rubbish," impacted my life in the same manner my Catholic upbringing spoke about suicide and talking to the dead. These subjects were taboo and sinful. Yet, I felt passion behind the spirit words and rehashed the phrase: *We have little voice; our love comes through the pen in physical reality.* My heart jumped several beats. Not sure if I reacted with fear or enthusiasm, but I knew someone needed to hear the words delivered by the spirits.

I learned to pray early in my life. Most of the time it involved repetition of litanies in the Catholic missal and catechism book. The rote recital of the verses often dragged mind and visual distractions into the prayers and drowned the words. Even though I spoke from my heart, it remained a one-way conversation with God. I never took the time to listen for a response although I understood and practiced active listening with people in my life. I didn't know to extend that same courtesy to the Creator.

Meditation never interested me before retirement. My life seemed too busy for a state of nothingness. Fortunately, my views changed.

Summary of the spirit messages for the survivors:

- *Healing the heart and emotional body takes courage, strength, love, and time.*

- *Self-doubt and blame initiate a shutdown of the mind. The ego or mind entertains and plays with our deepest fears and weaknesses. The spirits warn us to face our demons before they take our strength, claim victory, and shout, We have won.*

- *Pray from the heart. Bring in the light, feeling of oneness with all and connect with God. It heals and mends broken hearts.*

- *It is only when you release sorrow in your heart that both (the living and departed) are set free.*

- *We are all one, to each heart we (spirits) come to join.*

- *I love you. I am near. The swallows (departed souls) come back, to support and guide.*

- *Trust, love, and most important, live your life, true to yourself.*

- *"I'm so sorry," bellows souls who left the Earth plane too soon.*

The Night Watchmen communication exposed a depth of prayer and meditation that I hadn't experienced. In meditation, I asked for a more definitive explanation for the phrase, *Stop, reflect, and pray any way that you respect. We are all one.* The following reflects the answers to my questions in meditation.

"How do we pray, my Lord?" I asked.
"My child, how do you breathe the breath of life?
Make all your actions one of love, for the pure love of the soul is the breath of life in prayer.
Pray with the love of all your senses, actions, and thoughts."

"How do we still the mind, my Lord?"
"My dear, how do you still the breath?
When prayer becomes a natural reaction of your soul, your life becomes the breath of your soul.
When prayer becomes a natural fragrance of the soul, the spirit of love, God's love, becomes the breath of freedom, light, and grace."

"My Lord, how do we open the fountain of love, a gift from our Father and Creator?"
"See the beauty in all creation, the beauty of your soul, all that covers the Earthly plane.
Forget the anger, the torments of your mind.
Free the spirit within.
Let the love of mankind and all Earthly creation transform thoughts into love.
The love that exists within all."

The best and most beautiful things in the world
cannot be seen or even touched.
They must be felt with the heart.
Helen Keller

Resources

If you or someone you know is struggling with issues related to mental health, substance abuse, or suicidal thoughts, it's important to reach out for professional help. Here are some resources that can offer support:

Text or call 988. Available 24 hours a day.

1. **National Suicide Prevention Lifeline (US)** - A national network of local crisis centers that provides free and confidential emotional support to people in suicidal crisis or emotional distress twenty-four hours a day, seven days a week. The Lifeline can be reached at 1-800-273-TALK (1-800-273-8255). They also offer an online chat service.

2. **Crisis Text Line (US)** - A free, twenty-four seven text line for people in crisis. Text HOME to 741741 to communicate with a trained crisis counselor.

3. **Substance Abuse and Mental Health Services Administration (SAMHSA)** - Provides a confidential, free helpline, open twenty-four seven, 365 days a year, for individuals and family members facing mental and/or substance use disorders. This service provides referrals to local treatment facilities, support groups, and community-based organizations. 1-800-662-HELP (4357)

4. **NAMI (National Alliance on Mental Illness)** - The largest grassroots mental health organization dedicated to building better lives for millions of Americans affected by mental illness. They offer a free helpline for support and local referrals. 1-800-950-NAMI (6264)

5. **Befrienders Worldwide** - An international network of emotional support centers worldwide that provide support to people in emotional crisis or at risk of suicide through helplines. www.befrienders.org

6. **Mind (UK)** - Offers information and advice to people with mental health problems and lobbies government and local authorities on their behalf. Call 0300 123 3393 or text 86463

7. **Beyond Blue (Australia)** - Provides information and support to help everyone in Australia achieve their best possible mental health. Call 1300 22 4636

8. **Kids Help Phone (Canada)** - Canada's only twenty-four seven, national support service offering professional counseling, information, referrals, and volunteer-led, text-based support for young people. Call 1-800-668-6868 or text CONNECT to 686868

For mental health and suicide prevention resources specifically tailored to the LGBTQ community, several organizations offer specialized support, services, and information. Here are some prominent ones:

9. **The Trevor Project** - Provides crisis intervention and suicide prevention services to lesbian, gay, bisexual, transgender, queer & questioning (LGBTQ) young people under 25. They offer a 24/7 crisis hotline, chat, and text service. Call 1-866-488-7386 or text START 267-8678

10. **LGBT National Youth Talkline** - Provides telephone, online private one-to-one chat, and email peer-support, as well as information and local resources for cities and towns across the United States. 1-800-246-7743

11. **SAGE National LGBT Elder Hotline** - Offers older adults in the LGBTQ community a place to call when they need to talk about mental health concerns, find resources, or receive support. 1-877-360-5428

12. **Trans Lifeline**: www.translifeline.org

13. **LGBT National Help Center**: www.lgbthotline.org/national-hotline/

Veterans facing mental health challenges or seeking suicide prevention resources, there are dedicated organizations and programs designed to provide support, counseling, and crisis intervention. Here are some key resources:

14. **Veterans Crisis Line** - A 24/7 hotline available for veterans and their families. You can call, text, or chat to connect with qualified Department of Veterans Affairs responders. Call 1-800-273-8255 and press 1 or send a text to 838255.

15. **National Center for PTSD (Posttraumatic Stress Disorder)** - Part of the U.S. Department of Veterans Affairs, this center provides information, resources, and treatment options for PTSD among veterans. Call 1-802-296-6300, Email ncptsd@va.gov

16. **Military OneSource** - Offers a range of mental health resources, personal wellness coaching, and non-medical counseling for issues such as stress management, decision making, and relationship problems at no cost to active-duty, National Guard, and reserve members in any service branch. Call or Chat 1-800-342-9647

17. **Cohen Veterans Network** - A non-profit that provides high-quality, accessible, and integrated mental health services to veterans and their families, regardless of role or discharge status. Call 844-336-4226

Various religious and faith-based organizations offer support services for individuals struggling with suicidal thoughts, substance abuse, and grief. Many of these services incorporate spiritual guidance within the context of their religious beliefs.

18. **TheHopeLine** - An online platform that offers chat, email, and phone support. It provides faith-based hope and help for young people struggling with various issues, including thoughts of suicide and grief. www.thehopeline.com. Immediate help is provided at the National Suicide Prevention Hotline at 988.

19. **New Life Ministries** - Offers a network of Christian counselors and a variety of resources for those dealing with personal and family struggles, including suicide and substance abuse. 1-800-639-5433, www.newlife.com

20. **Saddleback Church's Hope for Mental Health Ministry** - Part of Pastor Rick Warren's church, this ministry offers support groups and resources for individuals and families affected by mental illness and suicide loss. 1-949-609-8000, www.saddleback.com

21. **American Association of Christian Counselors (AACC)** - Offers a directory of Christian counselors who provide support for a wide range of issues, including depression, suicide, and grief. 1-800-526-8673

22. **GriefShare** - A network of church-based grief recovery support groups that offer support to people experiencing grief and loss. www.griefshare.org, Call 1-800-395-5755, International 001-919-562-2112

23. **Jewish Family Services** - Jewish Family Services agencies often provide grief counseling and support that is open to people of all faiths, and they sometimes have specific programs for suicide prevention and support. 1-415-449-3700, www.jfcs.org

24. **Anthem of Hope** - A Christian mental health organization dedicated to amplifying hope for those battling brokenness, depression, anxiety, self-harm, addiction, and suicide. www.anthemofhope.org, 1-615-538-8374

Please note that these resources are region-specific and it's important to seek out support systems available in your own country and area if possible.

Always remember, you are not alone, and help is available.

Additional Resources

There are many books on the market that delve into the concept of communicating with spirits or channeling messages from the afterlife, offering guidance, comfort, and wisdom.

Many Lives, Many Masters by Dr. Brian Weiss. This book introduces the idea of past-life regression and messages from the Masters, or spiritual guides, who impart wisdom about life and the afterlife.

Journey of Souls by Michael Newton, PhD. Newton shares his case studies of individuals placed under hypnosis to reveal their experiences between lives, offering a unique perspective on what souls encounter in the afterlife.

Talking to Heaven: A Medium's Message of Life After Death by James Van Praagh. Van Praagh is a medium who provides accounts of his communications with spirits, offering comfort to those grieving, and a glimpse into the afterlife.

Wisdom from Your Spirit Guides by James Van Praagh. The book teaches readers the benefits and rewards of having a conscious relationship with their spirit guides. The book contains exercises and meditations to enrich and assist the reader's journey.

Messages from the Masters: Tapping into the Power of Love by Dr. Brian Weiss. Weiss uses his experience as a psychiatrist and hypnotherapist to share messages from the spirit realm about love and personal growth.

The Afterlife of Billy Fingers: How My Bad-Boy Brother Proved to Me There's Life After Death by Annie Kagan. Kagan recounts the messages she received from her deceased brother, offering insights into the afterlife and spiritual wisdom.

Afterlife Communication: 16 Proven Methods, 85 True Accounts by Gary Schwartz, Sonia Rinaldi, Suzanne Giesemann, Victor Zammit, Karen Herrick, Anne Puryear, Herb Puryear, Rochelle Wright,

Susanne Wilson, and Maria Pe. This book compiles various methods and accounts of afterlife communication, providing a range of perspectives and experiences.

Manifesting with the Angels by Charles Virtue. This is a guidebook that explores how individuals can use angelic guidance to enhance their ability to manifest their desires and personal goals.

Signs: The Secret Language of the Universe by Laura Lynne Jackson. Jackson, a psychic medium, shares stories and signs that she believes are communications from the beyond, aiming to show readers how the dead can interact with us.

At Heaven's Door by Williams J. Peters. This book illustrates powerful personal stories and convincing research of the many ways the living can and do accompany the dying into the afterlife.

Messengers of Light: The Angels' Guide to Spiritual Growth by Terry Lynn Taylor. The author shares how people can get in touch with angels, how to spot them, and how to utilize their help. Most importantly, Taylor shares how to love life the way angels do.

Each of these books provides a different approach to the concept of the afterlife and spirit communication, from scholarly research to personal narrative, and they often share a common goal of offering understanding and solace to readers curious about what might lie beyond death.

About the Author

Two years before Maureen Angelini retired from her career as a teacher and principal in public education, her life took a dramatic turn at the funeral of a friend who had died by suicide.

While she knelt gazing at the altar, she witnessed a fog appear above the casket and heard the haunting words in her mind, "I didn't know I would cause so much pain." This profound moment shattered her religious beliefs and understanding of the afterlife. Driven by an unquenchable thirst for answers, Maureen uncovered an innate ability to communicate with the spirit world.

Today she shares her experiences, the wisdom gained through her channeled communications, and the powerful messages of healing, hope, and love from those who have crossed over.

For more great books from Peak Press
Visit Books.GracePointPublishing.com

PEAK PRESS

If you enjoyed reading *Voices of Light* and purchased it through an online retailer, please return to the site and write a review to help others find the book.

www.ingramcontent.com/pod-product-compliance
Lightning Source LLC
Chambersburg PA
CBHW060134100426

42744CB00007B/784